MVSES

THE BOOK OF GODDESSES

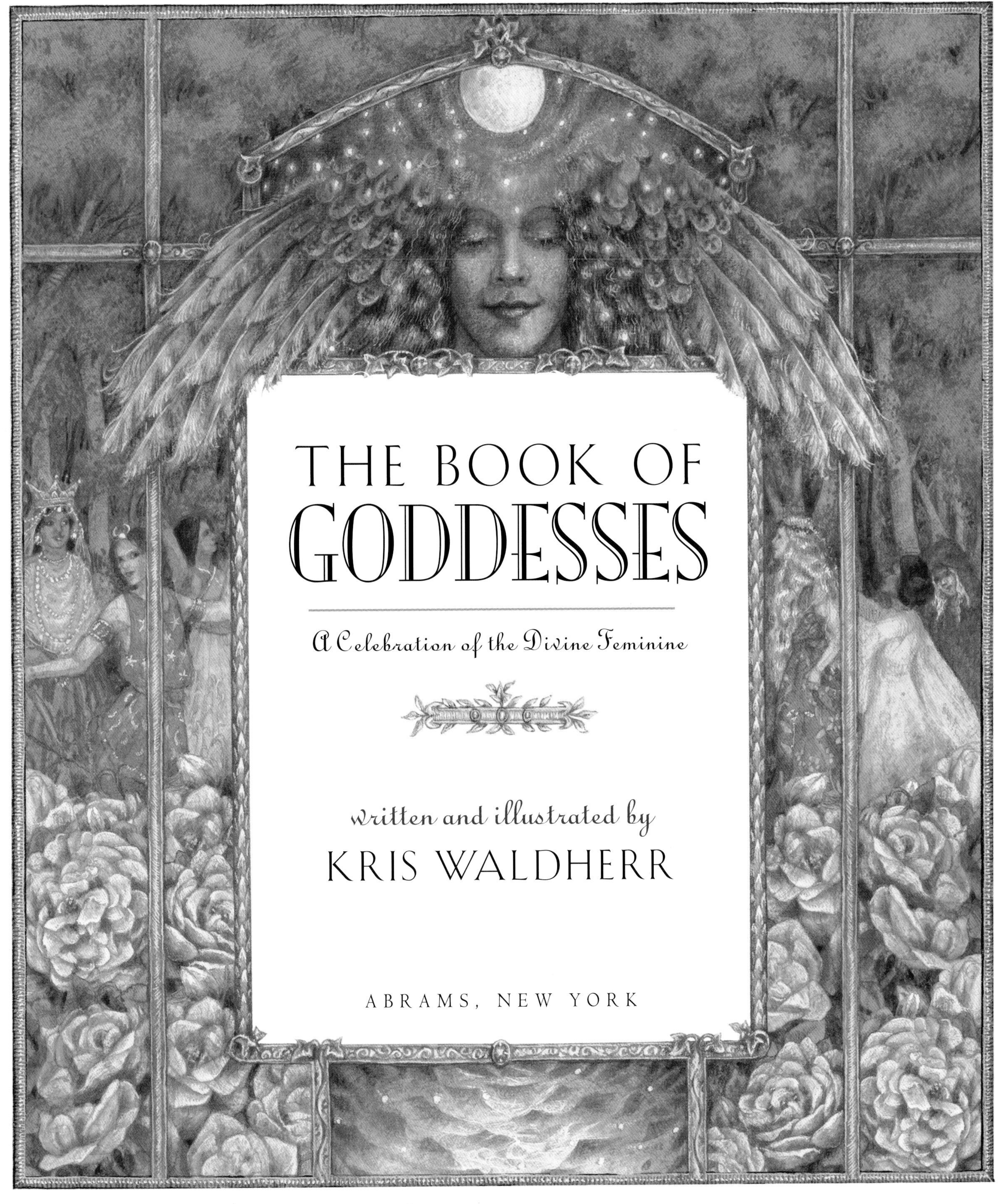

THE BOOK OF GODDESSES

A Celebration of the Divine Feminine

written and illustrated by

KRIS WALDHERR

ABRAMS, NEW YORK

For my daughter,
Thea Delphine,
with love

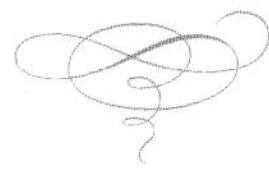

Designer: Kris Waldherr
Editor: Tamar Brazis
Production Manager: Kaija Markoe

Library of Congress Cataloging-in-Publication Data has been applied for.

ISBN 10: 0-8109-7054-6
ISBN 13: 978-0-8109-7054-0

Visit www.bookofgoddesses.com

Published in 2006 by Abrams, an imprint of Harry N. Abrams, Inc.

Printed and bound in Singapore
10 9 8 7 6 5 4 3 2 1

harry n. abrams, inc.
a subsidiary of La Martinière Groupe
115 West 18th Street
New York, NY 10011
www.hnabooks.com

CONTENTS

INTRODUCTION

IT ASTONISHES ME TO CONSIDER THAT IT HAS BEEN TEN YEARS since *The Book of Goddesses* was originally published. A decade is a weighty phase of time—to write it sounds substantial and stately. Yet, ten years is but a heartbeat in the life of the eternally Divine Feminine. By the Divine Feminine, I am referring to the unique wisdom and strength so many women possess in abundance; a quality so powerful, it can only be called divine.

For thousands of years around the globe, the Divine Feminine has been honored in the form of goddesses. The roles these goddesses play form a dizzying kaleidoscope of feminine sovereignty. One could call these goddesses and their qualities archetypes—primordial symbols held deep within our souls. As such, each of these goddess archetypes depicts the creative powers and talents women have always held. They also reflect the beliefs of the cultures who worshiped them, revealing what they revered and, in some cases, even feared in women.

One way the Divine Feminine was honored was in the form of a supreme triple goddess. The triple goddess, like the moon and her eternal phases, reflected women's different stages of life—the waxing moon symbolizing the young girl; the full moon, the fertile woman, or mother; and finally, the waning dark moon, the post-menstrual woman, who holds her "wise blood," or powers of creation, within herself. Some

scholars believe that, as humans became more sophisticated in their spiritual needs, these three goddesses splintered into many goddesses—all of whom represented different aspects of life, all of whom made up the Divine Feminine.

In this new and expanded edition of *The Book of Goddesses,* one hundred of these goddesses are presented in words and art. Also included here is most of the content of *Embracing the Goddess Within,* the sequel to *The Book of Goddesses.* By interweaving these two books, I aim to create a richly expansive portrait of the Divine Feminine—one which will encourage you to explore and celebrate the thousands of goddesses acknowledged throughout history. Some art in this edition has been presented in other books of mine, including *Persephone and the Pomegranate,* my retelling of perhaps the most important mother-daughter myth. In addition, new content has been expressively created for this volume. I am thankful for the opportunity to revisit subject matter so close to my heart.

The world is a different place than it was when *The Book of Goddesses* was first published ten years ago. While it has become less innocent, I'd like to think it has become more receptive to the life-affirming message of the Divine Feminine. It is with this renewed hope that I offer this anniversary edition of *The Book of Goddesses.* May it bring inspiration and empowerment to all aspects of your life.

—KRIS WALDHERR

PART ONE

BEGINNINGS

First in my prayer, before all other deities,
I call upon Gaia, Primeval Prophetess . . .
The Greek great earth mother.

AESCHYLUS

Tara

WHAT—OR WHO—COULD HAVE CREATED THE INFINITE complexity of connectiveness we call the universe? How did it all begin once upon a time? In this section, our exploration centers on some of the goddesses credited with creating the earth and universe. It also presents other divine women associated with creation. It is here that the Divine Feminine is perhaps at her most powerful and all-encompassing.

Like the creation goddesses acknowledged within these pages, as women we are all creatresses. As such, we reflect the universe within ourselves and our bodies. With our bodies, we can give birth to life. With our hearts and minds, we can give birth to works that can change the world. Using this equation, is it any wonder so many goddesses are honored as the Great Mother?

ASIA
AFRICA

GAIA

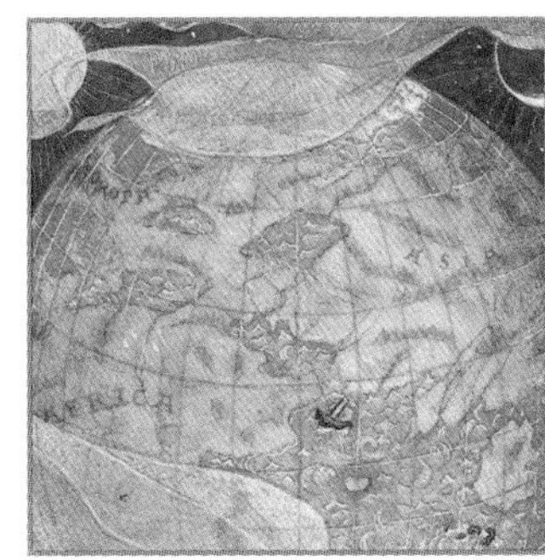

What could have existed before the earth? It is difficult to imagine—our minds and senses are irrevocably entwined with our experiences of life upon this planet. The beauty of our green and blue world, with its many forms of life, has a magnificence that warrants our respectful protection.

For thousands of years and in cultures all around the world, the earth has been worshiped in one form or another. In ancient Greece, the earth was personified as a mysterious goddess called Gaia. A cosmic, procreative womb who emerged out of the primeval void called Chaos, it was believed Gaia existed before all other life. It was also believed that Gaia created all of life. In Roman mythology, she was known as Terra.

At her famed shrine at Delphi, Gaia was honored by priestesses who threw sacred herbs into a cauldron, using the fragrant smoke to invoke the goddess's eternal wisdom. Later, the sun god Apollo was worshiped at Delphi. Orpheus, the famed musician son of Apollo, was credited with this beautiful hymn in praise of Gaia:

Oh Goddess, Source of Gods and Mortals,
All-Fertile, All-Destroying Gaia,
Mother of All, Who brings forth the bounteous fruits and flowers,
All variety, Maiden who anchors the eternal world in our own,
Immortal, Blessed, crowned with every grace,
Deep bosomed Earth, sweet plains and fields, fragrant grasses in the nurturing rains,
Around you fly the beauteous stars, eternal and divine. . . .

CELESTIAL CREATION

Though Gaia was powerful unto herself, she did not choose a solitary existence. Gaia formed from her womb the sea, which she called Pontus, and the sky, which she called Uranus. She took Uranus as her husband, to keep her company and to make love with. Sky lying upon earth created numerous children within the goddess's great womb. Uranus, fearful they would prove more powerful than he, would not allow Gaia to give birth to them.

In time, Gaia grew uncomfortable with life. But then the goddess thought of a solution to her dilemma: She gave her youngest and strongest child, Kronos, or Time, a sickle made of a steely diamond-like material called adamantine, which he used to cut Uranus's genitals from the portal of her womb. Uranus's blood fell upon the earth, and merged with it to create further offspring: the Furies, the Giants, and the Nymphs. And so, sky was freed from earth, thus giving birth to the universe.

After Uranus was separated from Gaia, she had other children, these fathered by Pontus, the sea. In this way Gaia created all the gods and goddesses of the Greek world, creating order where Chaos once reigned.

The myth of Gaia reminds us of the interconnection of the world—and the importance of living in harmony with its resources, as well as our fellow humans. To experience this harmony in our lives is the greatest gift we can hope to receive.

SPIDER WOMAN

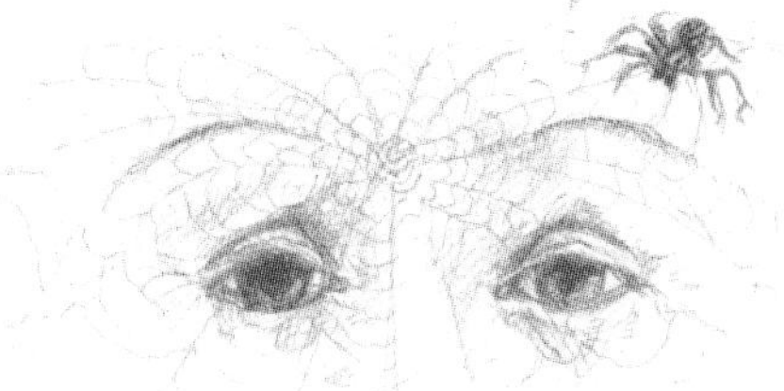

Many cultures around the world believe that all of the world's creatures are connected by a strong, but delicately woven, web. The Pueblo Indians credit the spinning of this web of life to a creation goddess so potent that her true name is never spoken aloud. Some call this goddess Spider Woman. She is also honored as Thought Woman, because everything was created from her thoughts.

Spider Woman existed before the world existed. By spinning and chanting, she was able to create the four directions of the universe—north, south, east, and west. Within this sacred space, she produced her daughters, Ut Set and Nau Ut Set. Following their mother's directions carefully, Ut Set and Nau Ut Set made the sun, moon, and stars to banish darkness from the universe; they created these heavenly bodies from shells, turquoise, red rock, yellow stone, and clear crystal.

As she spun her web, Spider Woman made all of life, including the mountains, lakes, oceans, and deserts. She also created the different races of people from differently colored clays. Finally, using a last thread of her web, Spider Woman connected each human being to her always.

Other Native American traditions acknowledge Spider Woman. She is a creatress to the Pima and Zia Indians. The Navajo believe she taught them how to weave. Among the Hopi Indians, who settled in what is now known as Arizona, she was one of the deities who created Poquanghoya and Palongawhoya; these powerful twins created the earth, with its bountiful fields, seas, and mountains.

OPENING THE DOORWAY

Spider Woman's magical thread is referenced by feminist scholar Merlin Stone in her book *Ancient*

Mirrors of Womanhood. Stone writes that each of us has a doorway at the top of our head that joins us to Spider Woman. In yogic traditions, this doorway is called the crown chakra, a place of energy associated with the highest spiritual enlightenment. To invoke the creative wisdom of Spider Woman, all we need to do is open our doorway and take note of the precious thread connecting us to her web.

Like Spider Woman as she spun her web, one way to open this doorway is with music or chanting. This technique has been used by shamans around the globe to bring about a transcendental state of mind. In Siberia, the shaman performed music by straddling his or her drum and beating it, as if the drum were a steed transporting them to the faraway place of the spirits.

Many Native American traditions also include ceremonial drumming as a means of reaching this heightened state of consciousness. Their practices live on today—as does the memory of Spider Woman, creatress of the universe.

TARA

The most important deity for Tibetan Buddhists is the compassionate mother goddess Tara. They believe that Tara has the power to heal all sorrows and grant all wishes. The name Tara translates into English as "she who causes one to cross," which means that the goddess will help her devotees cross safely to the other side of a troublesome situation.

Tibetan Buddhists approach life as a process that grants them opportunities to gain wisdom. They believe that wisdom leads to true happiness and peace—a treasure greater than any riches the world can offer. Such an enlightened person is called a Buddha, or "blessed one."

Tara was believed to be a mortal woman who yearned to become the first female Buddha. One story claims that to reach this goal, she worked and prayed for the welfare of humans everywhere for over ten million years. Then she was transformed into a goddess whose only desire was to ease the world's pain.

Tara is depicted at different times with differently colored skins, suggesting her many realms of influence. She is most popularly seen as White Tara and Green Tara. As White Tara, the goddess bears skin as brilliant as the truth itself. Renowned for her compassion, White Tara is called the mother of all Buddhas. Green Tara, who appears as a young teenage girl, is thinner in figure than White Tara; she is believed to grant wishes to her most loyal devotees. Other colors the goddess takes on include red, yellow, orange, and blue.

THE PROTECTRESS

Tara is honored as the protectress against the many fears that block men and women from living in harmony. Stories about Tara often reveal the concerns of the people of old Tibet. For example,

the goddess is believed to protect her followers from the fear of elephants, poisonous snakes, and lions.

One ancient legend tells how she saved a wood-gatherer from a vicious lioness. When the wood-gatherer called for help, Tara suddenly appeared to him, dressed in forest leaves, and pulled him from the hungry jaws of the lioness. Then she returned the man safely to the marketplace. Her work done, she mysteriously disappeared.

But other fears from which Tara offers protection are those that anyone can identify with. Who has never felt the fear of poverty, unfair imprisonment, or theft? Or the temptation of pride, doubt, and envy? Tara will not only protect her followers, but she will also save all those who cry her name at the moment of their suffering.

Tara is Tibet's most popular deity. She is still widely worshiped today.

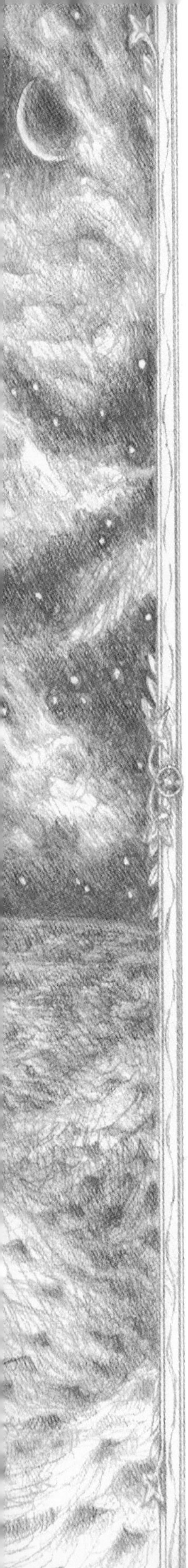

ADITI

In India, Aditi is honored as the creator of life, a Hindu goddess of infinite vastness who held dominion over everything. It was Aditi who gave birth to all of the gods and goddesses; they in turn brought everything to consciousness. Some believe that this benign deity predated the Vedic period, which began around 1500 BCE. She was originally acknowledged as a primordial great goddess who controlled the past and the future.

Aditi is called the Cow of Light—she nurtures the world, just as cows nourish humans with their gift of milk. This honorific also suggests a connection to the Milky Way, the band of stars that illuminates the night sky. Aditi is also addressed as Mother Space because she gave birth to the planets and stars.

ENDLESS SKY

It is impossible for humans to fully comprehend the infinity of the universe. This vast space, filled with teeming life and light, is immeasurable. It comprises the celestial realm of Aditi, Mother Space. Appropriately, Aditi's name translates literally as "limitless." In later years, the goddess was thought to represent the endless sky, which wraps itself around all of existence.

Cloaked with the sun, Aditi was said to glisten with brilliance and benevolence. Her children, who were fathered by the god Kashyapa, were known collectively as the Adityas. These solar *devas,* or divine beings, were thought to protect their supplicants from illness, and were associated with the twelve months of the year. They also symbolized the twelve spirits of the zodiac, whom some believe control fate. One story promises that the Adityas would reveal themselves fully at Doomsday, when all truth is made known.

ERDA

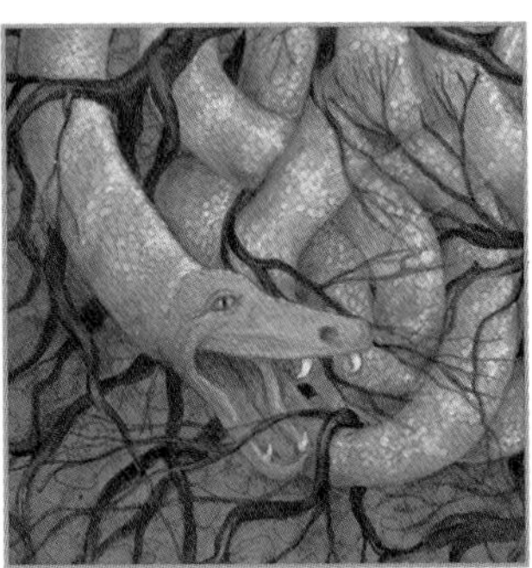

The Norse earth goddess, Erda, was believed to live in a cave within the earth's deepest recesses, which was set next to the roots of Yggdrasil, the vast World Tree. The earth was thought to revolve on its axis around Yggdrasil, whose massive limbs sustained and connected all of life. Yggdrasil was watered by Erda's plentiful fountain of wisdom. This pure source of water enabled the tree's tallest branches to reach the heavens, and its widest branches to give shade to all.

Erda's powers were as encompassing as Yggdrasil's leafy span—indeed, the goddess and her magical fountain were often invoked by those in need of her far-reaching wisdom. Others believed Erda could bend the inexorable powers of fate, over which she ruled. One myth tells how the Norse god Odin gave up one of his eyes for the privilege of drinking from Erda's fountain; his quest for knowledge was worth more to him than the pedestrian gift of eyesight.

Another story claims that Erda is the oldest goddess of the three Norns, a trio of sister goddesses associated with the past, present, and future. They were believed to help mothers as they gave birth, and ruled over a person's unchangeable destiny.

DIVINING FATE

Because of Erda's association with fate, the Norse believed there was a clear correlation between the goddess and the art of divination, a valued part of pre-Christian Scandinavian society. It may be hard to imagine today, but at that time, every home was open to seeresses—female practitioners of the art of divination, who were believed to receive help from the spirit world. The predictions presented by the seeress often came in the form of mysterious poems obtained by the use of runes, or other oracles whose messages she was skilled in deciphering.

The seeress made her runes from bone or wood strips cut from a nut-bearing tree, upon which potent symbols were carved or painted. In a way, by creating runes from a tree, the seeress was drawing from that same fountain of wisdom Erda used to nurture Yggdrasil and, consequently, invoking the goddess herself.

The Norse also turned to the earth itself for guidance. They used many aspects of it as oracles—animals, birds, the sky, even the ocean—believing that the observation of these things could bring divine answers to questions posed. Horses in particular were considered to be the confidants of the gods and goddesses, able to reveal heaven's will to sensitive humans. A horse's calm movements could promise a peaceful solution to the questions posed; other movements mirrored other outcomes.

Using natural forms as oracles reminds us that the earth can give us the answers we need to our most urgent and primal queries. By using these forms of divinations, the Norse were able to receive wisdom directly from Erda, Mother Earth.

CHANG O

Around the world, the moon is associated with numerous objects. The fanciful believe it is made of cheese because of its pocked surface. Others claim to see the face of a man in the moon if they gaze closely enough. In China, the moon is associated with a celestial white rabbit, who is said to reside there with the goddess Chang O.

Before Chang O became a moon goddess, she lived with her husband, Yi, and the other gods and goddesses. Yi was honored as the divine archer and was proud of his unsurpassed skill—so much so that he shot nine suns out of the sky, leaving only one to warm the earth. As punishment, the couple were stripped of their immortality and forced to live among humans.

Chang O was dismayed at their humiliation. She begged her husband to seek the potion of immortality from the goddess Hsi Wang Mu, who concocted it from magical peaches. Hsi Wang Mu was sympathetic. She gave Yi enough for the couple to become immortal, but not enough to become divine.

When Yi returned, Chang O was initially delighted by his success. But Yi did not want to drink the potion straightaway. Instead, he told his wife to watch over it while he went hunting.

As time passed and Chang O waited for her husband to return, she became more and more agitated. Then she had an idea: If she drank Yi's potion as well as her own, perhaps she would become a goddess again. After all, she reasoned, she was not the one who had shot down the sun, so why should she be punished? Too tempted to resist, she drank it all.

Chang O soon felt herself becoming lighter and lighter. She floated away from earth toward the heavens. More quickly than Chang O thought possible, she landed on the moon, once again a beautiful goddess—but unable to leave because of her weightlessness.

Though Yi was at first angry with Chang O, he did love her; he quickly forgave her when he saw how lonely she was. To make her more comfortable on the cold moon, Yi built her a magnificent palace out of fragrant cinnamon wood, and brought her a white rabbit for companionship. Their marriage continued, but it was limited: Yi was only able to visit his wife once a month during the full moon—the night when moon meets the sun's rays.

TASTING IMMORTALITY

Every September, when the full moon is at its most brilliant, the Chinese honor Chang O with a moon festival. This festival also celebrates women and features family reunions. Besides gathering to admire the moon's luminescent brilliance, people bake special, round treats called moon cakes, which are filled with delicious red bean paste. As people eat them, they are reminded of Chang O, queen of the moon.

One story from China's past suggests the power of these delectable pastries to influence history. During the oppressive Yuan dynasty, which existed during the fourteenth century, a brave rebel named Liu Fu Tong used moon cakes to incite a revolution. With no way to communicate without gaining notice, Liu Fu Tong hid small pieces of paper within moon cakes, bearing the date that the rebels would rise against the Yuan dynasty to take back control. He gave them to his fellow warriors, who discovered the secret message once they cut the cakes in two.

Their surprise revolution was successful. Thus, Liu Fu Tong was able to transform his native land—just as Chang O was transformed by the potion of immortality.

HATHOR

Hathor was honored in ancient Egypt as the Golden One—a divinity powerful enough to help worshipers with dilemmas ranging from love difficulties to the lack of prosperity. A goddess of fertility and plenty, she was believed to be mother to the pantheon of Egyptian gods and goddesses.

Hathor was also called the Celestial Cow because of her ability to nurture the entire world. She was often depicted with the face of a cow, or wearing a headdress of horns with a circle—representing the sun—resting above. More rarely, she was shown bearing the form of a cobra, lioness, or hippopotamus.

Public festivals to honor Hathor were held in November. These rituals often consisted of the ceremonial carrying and display of the sacred statues of the Celestial Cow. Many also identify this goddess with the Milky Way, that beautiful band of stars so visible on dark, moonless nights. Appropriately, Hathor was also honored as the Mistress of Heaven.

Hathor was so popular that at one point she was served by as many as sixty-one priestesses in her sacred temple. She was especially beloved in Ta-Netjer in Upper Egypt. Sculptures of Hathor's face, adorned with cow ears, were often placed at the top of temple columns. Even today, her shrines are still visited by women seeking assistance with the conception of children.

THE PROMISE OF PLENTY

From the earliest times, Hathor was petitioned for assistance in creating personal abundance, such as help with a love affair. Rituals also invoked her for communal abundance, as in the creation of a generous harvest to feed everyone.

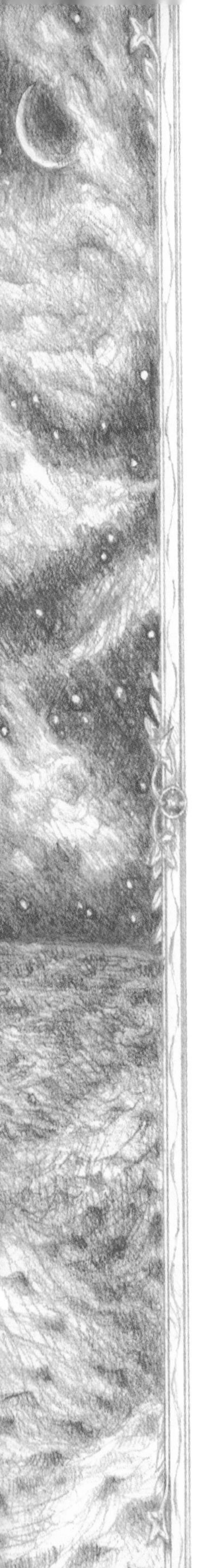

One ritual involved leading cows out to fields to be milked. Their new milk would then be poured upon the hungry ground in libation to the goddess. This ritual would be performed in hopes of persuading Hathor to send nurturing rain to help the crops grow. A similar but simpler ritual performed by the Egyptians to please Hathor used magically charged water, which was also sprinkled upon the earth.

These acts were done with the intention of creating sympathetic magic. This is the belief that an action performed on a smaller scale can create the hoped-for outcome by magically reflecting it—just as the Celestial Cow reflected the plenty of the universe.

Chang O

RELATED GODDESSES

AMATERASU

A benevolent solar goddess, Amaterasu is the supreme deity of Shintoism, a religion practiced primarily in Japan. One myth concerns her anger with her brother, the storm god. To punish him, the goddess hid herself in a cave, thus plunging the world into darkness. Balance was restored when Amaterasu was lured out and entranced by her reflection in a strategically placed mirror.

ASTARTE

This Assyrian goddess is one of the most ancient deities honored by humanity; her shrines date from the Neolithic age. Honored as the Queen of Heaven, Astarte was thought to rule over stars, who were believed to be the brightly shining spirits of the dead.

BILIKU

In the Andaman Islands in India, the creation goddess Biliku often appears in the form of a spider. Considered to be both benevolent and malevolent, Biliku was believed to be the first deity to own and control fire.

BIRRA NULA

In Australian Aboriginal mythology, Birra nula is considered a creation deity. She is also married to Baiame, the ruling god who resides in the Milky Way. This goddess is associated with Birrahgnooloo, a water goddess who is also thought to be a wife of Baiame.

Mama Quilla

Besides being a goddess of marriage, Mama Quilla was an Incan moon divinity; her name translates as "Mother Moon." As such, she was associated with calendars. One story claims that she was the mother of the first Incan.

Nügua

This ancient Chinese goddess was believed to bear the tail of a dragon; in the Chinese tradition, dragons are considered very fortuitous. To ease her loneliness, Nügua fashioned the first humans from clay. Because of this act, she was honored as a creator of life.

Nut

This mother goddess was worshiped by the ancient Egyptians as the physical personification of the night sky. Paintings depict her as a naked woman covered in stars, her body sharply arched over the earth in protection. One story relates that the sun god, Re, was reborn each morning from her womb.

Shakti

The goddess Shakti is honored in several ways in India. According to Tantric tradition, Shakti is the powerful feminine counterbalance to masculine energy. In the Vedic religion, she is a goddess of sexuality and the beloved consort of Shiva, Lord of the Dance. Shakti's name translates as "Divine Energy"—an appropriate honorific for a deity who animates all of life.

White Buffalo Woman

The Lakota people believe that White Buffalo Woman descended from the heavens in the form of a beautiful woman to teach them their way of life. She gave them several important religious ceremonies, and revealed the colors of the four directions of the earth. Before departing, she transformed into a supernatural white buffalo calf.

PART TWO

LOVE

In that meadow where horses have grown glossy,
and all spring flowers grow wild,
the anise shoots fill the air with aroma.
And here our queen Aphrodite pours
celestial nectar in the gold cups.

SAPPHO

Venus

PERSEPHONE AND HER FIRST LOVE. VENUS'S PASSION AND sensuality. Benzai-ten's serene, transcendent love that accepts all. Seductive, flirtatious, noble, beautiful, warm, and cool—all-goddess, all-divine, and all-knowing of heartbreak and joy without end.

As there are experiences of passionate love, so there are goddesses to represent our personal experiences. The goddesses presented in this section suggest the grand movement of our transformation from innocence toward wisdom, girl into woman.

How fortunate for us that the passage of time allows us opportunities to savor different types of love relationships! Whether these relationships are with a lover, partner, or spouse, short-term or lasting through eternity, all love relationships offer joys and challenges. They reflect the yearning of the Divine Feminine for her beloved consort.

VENUS

Venus was the name the ancient Romans gave to the goddess of love. Created from the union of sea and sky, Venus was born of sea foam and water, and brought to earth upon a conch shell. She was described as "the star of the sea" by her worshipers, and considered the queen of pleasure.

Venus is the goddess who inspires people to love each other, ensuring that the human race continues to grow. For hundreds of years, artists and poets have turned to her for inspiration. The Italian artist Botticelli painted a magnificent picture called *The Birth of Venus*; the playwright and poet William Shakespeare wrote her praises in his poem *Venus and Adonis*.

As the unwilling wife of Vulcan, the crippled god of forging and handicrafts, Venus serves to represent the necessary balance of beauty with utilitarianism. But a goddess of such overwhelming beauty and sensuality could not be loyal to one so ugly—many were those whom the goddess favored with her affections. Included among them was Mars, the god of war, and Adonis, who broke Venus's heart when he was killed by a boar. It was with a mortal man, Anchises, that Venus gave birth to her son, Aeneas. Through Aeneas, Venus came to be honored as the mother of the Roman people.

Aeneas was a Trojan prince who escaped after the fall of Troy and sailed to Italy, where he became the founder of Rome. During his many adventures, which were recorded in *The Aeneid* by the poet Virgil, Aeneas was protected by enchanted armor that his goddess mother persuaded Vulcan to make for him.

Shrines have been built to Venus in many parts of the Mediterranean. Some think that the city of Venice, in northern Italy, is named after her. Each year the people of Venice celebrate the marriage of their city to the sea by throwing a golden wedding ring into the Venetian lagoon. This ceremony ensures that the city will continue to be blessed with prosperity.

Venus was known to the Greeks as Aphrodite; Aphrodite's name translates literally as "she who comes from the foam." Her attendants, three Graces named Joyous, Brilliance, and Flowering, illustrate the wonders the goddess can offer, if she chooses to smile upon our earthly petitions.

ROMANTIC LOVE

Images of sensuality and romance abound in Venus's myths. On the island of Cyprus, where the goddess Aphrodite was believed to first set foot upon earth, shellfish were sacred due to their similarity in shape to a woman's vulva. The rose, Venus's special flower, was the object of desire in medieval quest romances, understood to symbolize the velvety folds of a woman's most precious and private jewel.

The scent of myrtle, also sanctified to Venus, bespoke of love and attraction; brides of the Greco-Roman world wore wreaths of it on their wedding day. The poet Ovid wrote that Venus was worshiped at the Veneralia, a festival celebrated every April first. For this holiday, Ovid claimed women must "wash the statues of Venus all over, put their golden necklaces on again, and give them roses and other flowers; and then, as the goddess commands, you must wash yourself under the green myrtle." The number six and the color pink are also associated with the goddess of love.

But it was Cestus, the goddess's richly embroidered girdle or belt, that held her most powerful spell. This magical length of cloth could make the wearer seductive enough to bewitch even the most unyielding of lovers into romantic congress.

Many of these stories can be easily seen in our current courtship rituals. Instead of worshiping conch shells, we feed our lovers oysters and whisper to them about the quickening of sexual prowess. We bring roses for Valentine's Day. We scent ourselves with sweet perfumes, and we dress with special care to look our most enchanting. All of these acts enable us to invite Venus, goddess of love, into our lives today.

RATI

Worshiped in India, beautiful Rati bears the ripe body of a heavily pregnant woman. Her passion-inspiring powers share similarities with Venus, the Roman goddess of love. Rati is one of the wives of Kama, the god of desire, whom some compare to Cupid, the desire-creating son of Venus. Kama was born of Lakshmi, the beloved Hindu goddess of prosperity, and Vishnu, the powerful god known as the preserver.

Though Rati was daughter to the fiery sun god Daksha, she is associated with water. The Apsaras—a group of water goddesses as changeable as the tide—include this Hindu love goddess among their many members. Renowned for their bewitching, shapeshifting powers, the Apsaras often take on the appearance of seductive women, with long, dark hair heavily perfumed with sandalwood. They are impossible to resist, and can tempt the celibate to give up their solitary ways. Some believe these enchantresses serve as attendants to Kama.

Rati is also honored on the Indonesian island of Bali. There she appears as a large-breasted woman, her vulva-like mouth twisted in erotic abandon. In this form, the goddess suggests overwhelming sexuality—a force too powerful to resist.

PASSION'S MUSE

The Hindu faith views sex as a spiritual, pleasurable activity—an important practice that should not be shamefully hidden from other aspects of life. Much art and literature exists to encourage the full enjoyment of romantic congress. Perhaps the most famous book devoted to this subject is the *Kama Sutra,*

which was written during the Gupta period (320 to 550 CE) in Indian history. The fame of the *Kama Sutra* expanded far beyond India, and it is still consulted to this day.

Rati served as inspiration for a similar text, entitled the *Ratirahasya*; the name of this book means "the secrets of love." The love goddess's secrets are exposed within its explicit pages, which include numerous techniques to bring lovers pleasure. Many of the sexual positions detailed in the *Ratirahasya* bear Rati's name upon them. They suggest her divine involvement—and approval—of the physical manifestations of love.

PERSEPHONE

Persephone, the treasured daughter of the harvest goddess Demeter, was honored by the ancient Greeks as the queen of the underworld. Her transformational journey from sunny earth to dark Hades was instigated when Pluto, god of death, fell in love with her.

One day, as Persephone gathered blossoms in a meadow, the earth suddenly split in two beneath her feet. Out of the abyss leapt a gold chariot pulled by black horses. Its driver was Pluto. He seized Persephone by the waist as the chariot raced back into the center of the earth.

Deep in the underworld and far from her mother, Persephone was forced to wed Pluto. The girl's heart was unmoved by the god's declarations of devotion. Instead, she wept for Demeter and refused to eat. Finally, after some time had passed, Persephone deigned to taste six seeds of the pomegranate. This act defined the goddess's life, for it symbolized Persephone's reluctant acceptance of her sexuality and of Pluto as her husband. It also ensured her separation from her mother, Demeter, for half of the year—a month for each seed tasted. This myth was used by the ancient Greeks to explain the turn of the seasons.

With its many clusters of seeds, the pomegranate is a rich allegory for the fruitfulness of a woman's ovaries. Indeed, many paintings from the Renaissance portray the Virgin Mary surrounded by pomegranates to suggest her life-giving force. For some women, Persephone's sojourn into the underworld can also represent the dark, depressive underworld of their psyche—a place many do not encounter until sexual maturity.

FIRST BLOOD, FIRST LOVE

The mysterious myth of Persephone is in many ways the story of a girl's initiation into the meaning of her blood—the menstrual blood that holds the secret of sexual ripening. Few women are emotionally ready to be sexually active at the time of their first flow. However, it is this first blood that shows us that this time is not far off—soon we will fall in love with another and choose to share our bodies with them.

The miraculous power of first menstruation is something our society has few rituals to commemorate, though other less industrialized cultures do. Like Persephone's descent into the sunless underworld, these initiation rituals usually included the segregation of the menstruating woman to a hut used solely for this purpose; no light was allowed to enter its darkened interior. Men, having no equivalent to menstruation, often created rituals to mirror what happens naturally to women. Tribes in Australia knock out a boy's tooth at puberty, creating a bleeding mouth. Other cultures practice subcision, an operation that splits the penis lengthwise to resemble a vulva.

The main rituals associated with Persephone are the great Eleusinian mysteries. Little is known of them. However, one thing is certain: Those who underwent the rites of Eleusis were changed irrevocably. The poet Cicero wrote of them, "We have been given a reason not only to live in joy, but also to die with better hope."

The Eleusinian mysteries took place every September in Athens. Some believe that at one time these secret rites allowed only women as participants. The rites began with the initiates fasting for nine days. At the end of this time, they purified themselves in the ocean and proceeded by foot to Eleusis, a walk that took most of the day. Once there, the initiates were covered with cloth and were brought into the temple.

It is uncertain what happened after this. Some say that the blindfolded initiates were led through maze-like passageways; others believe they were shown a sheaf of grain, which represented Persephone's return from the underworld, as well as Demeter's miraculous life-creating powers. When the initiates were led back to the world of light, they broke their fast with *kykeon*, a drink of water and mint thickened by meal.

Today, we still remember Persephone as the first aspect of the triple goddess—the *kore*, or maiden, who will become a mother and a crone one day. As our first blood transforms us from girl to woman, we acknowledge her presence within ourselves.

OSHUN

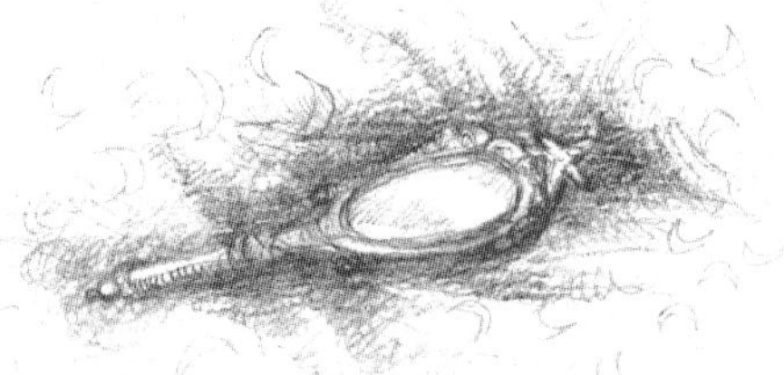

The Yoruba goddess Oshun is as sparkling as the African river that bears her name. Oshun's exotic beauty is intoxicating—her dark skin is as sleek as velvet; her elaborate headdress made of richly hued feathers to set off her brilliant eyes.

Worshiped in both Africa and the Caribbean, flirtatious Oshun is a popular goddess for those wishing to attract love. The fertility of women, a product of love, falls under her many concerns as a water deity. In Nigeria, women honor her with the Ibo-Osun, a ceremony that includes dancing and a feast featuring yams. The goddess is also one of the wives of Chango, the powerful Yoruba thunder god, with whom she is said to have borne human children.

Oshun is also noted as a healer and associated with wealth. In Puerto Rico, she is symbolized by a pumpkin—a fruit as bright in color as a shiny coin.

THE SENSUALITY OF LUXURY

Love encourages all forms of sensuality, which bring pleasure into our lives. Oshun represents the sensual luxury that wealth can create—richly decorated homes, flattering clothing, sweet-smelling perfumes. These luxuries help us become more receptive to love, by softening our hearts with beauty.

Though known as the Modest One, Oshun nonetheless delights in adorning herself. To make her desirable to her beloved, the goddess dresses herself with gleaming jewels, ornaments made of brass and yellow copper, and luxurious silks. The peacock, a bird noted for its showy plumage, is associated with Oshun. Some believe she wears seven bracelets upon her graceful arm, along with a mirror attached to her belt to better view her divine beauty.

PSYCHE

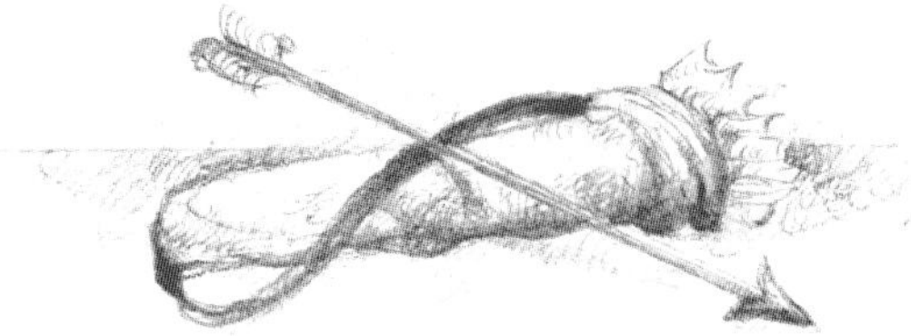

In classical Greece and Rome, the goddess Psyche began her life as a mortal woman whose unworldly beauty won her divinity—as well as the love of a god more powerful than any. Psyche symbolizes the woman's soul as love transforms her from innocence to wisdom; the Greek word for both "butterfly" and "soul" is *psyche*. Psyche is often depicted with the translucent wings of a butterfly, suggesting her transformation from mortal girl to goddess. After the ultimate transformation of death, many traditions hold that the spirit leaves the body in the form of a butterfly or moth.

The goddess Psyche is best known for her association with Cupid, the handsome son of Venus; Cupid's name is derived from *cupido,* the Latin word for "desire." Psyche's transformation from mortal girl to woman goddess began when Cupid fell in love with her against his will.

LOVE'S TRANSFORMATION

Since Psyche's birth, men and women had hailed her as a new goddess because of her beauty. These attentions also brought her the angry notice of Venus, the Roman goddess of love. When mortals neglected her temples to honor Psyche instead, Venus took revenge. She asked Cupid to visit Psyche while she slept and pierce her with one of his magic arrows. After waking, the girl would burn with a foolish lust for the first thing she might see.

Though Cupid had heard the praises of Psyche's beauty, his hands shook upon seeing the beauty asleep. An arrow poised in his bow slipped, grazing his thigh. From that moment, Cupid loved Psyche and wanted her above all others. Unable to act on his desire because of his mother's jealousy, Cupid visited the girl each night as she slept.

Weeks passed and Psyche remained unaware of the god of love's attentions. Then Psyche's parents decided it was time that she marry. Months passed and no suitor asked Psyche for her hand. In desperation, her parents consulted the oracle of Apollo. Animals were sacrificed, their bones thrown and read by the priests. All the signs led to one message: No mortal man would be Psyche's husband. Instead, she would be abandoned upon a cliff where a monster would claim her as his bride. Everyone wept at the news, for surely this meant Psyche's death.

But something unexpected occurred once Psyche was left alone to await her husband. Soft winds cradled the girl, carrying her to a faraway island where a palace stood. In its darkest chamber, Psyche was met by an unseen man who embraced her as his wife. When she awoke in the morning, he was gone.

Apart from the world, Psyche's husband continued to visit her each night in the darkness. She was content, for he was kind and loving. But in time, Psyche carried a child within her; her satisfaction turned to doubt as she remembered the oracle's frightening prediction. What if she gave birth to a monster who would slay her upon his emergence from her womb? She decided she had to know who she had married—even if this knowledge destroyed her happiness.

One night Psyche's curiosity got the better of her. She waited until her husband fell asleep, lit a lamp, and stole a look at him. No beast greeted her eyes—only the radiant Cupid. Psyche's hands shook, spilling hot oil onto him. Injured, the love god awoke and disappeared in a rage, ignoring the girl's profuse apologies.

While Cupid's anger quickly cooled, Venus's did not. The goddess made Psyche perform a series of daunting tasks to prove herself worthy of her son. With a little divine help, the girl completed them all and was reunited with her husband—and transformed into a goddess. In time, their child, a daughter named Pleasure, was born in the brilliant presence of the gods and goddesses of Olympus.

BENZAI-TEN

The most beloved figures in Japanese mythology are those who form a group known as the Seven Gods of Good Fortune. Of these seven deities, the fairy-like Benzai-ten is the sole goddess. Many Japanese prints and sculptures show Benzai-ten and her fellow Gods of Good Fortune sailing merrily together on a treasure ship.

Humans find happiness in many ways. For some people, happiness comes from gaining wisdom and knowledge; others find joy in beauty, music, and art. Benzai-ten is the goddess of all these gifts. She is believed to bring happiness and wealth to her worshipers—appropriately, the middle syllable of her name, *zai,* means "talent" or "wealth" in Japanese. Sometimes this goddess is depicted with eight arms bearing open hands, symbolizing her many talents and all-embracing generosity.

Though human in form, Benzai-ten was the daughter of a dragon king. She agreed to wed a child-devouring dragon in exchange for his promise to stop eating them. Upon their marriage, the dragon lost his appetite for children—his love for the goddess had healed his beastly temperament, transforming him into a model husband. Many people believe that Benzai-ten lives with her dragon-husband under the waves of Lake Biwa, which is north of the ancient city of Kyoto. The lake is named after Benzai-ten's favorite instrument, the *biwa,* a stringed instrument which is like a mandolin; the shape of the lake is similar to that of the *biwa.*

Stories tell of Benzai-ten's sympathy for young men under attack by dragons. Due to her close ties with those ferocious creatures, this goddess is able to help the men escape with their lives. Other tales praise Benzai-ten's kindness to lovers. Those who seek her help with love often leave beseeching letters upon this lovely goddess's shrines. Due to this, Benzai-ten is also considered a goddess of marriage.

TO KNOW THE BELOVED

In many romantic relationships, once love's first infatuation begins its necessary turn toward reality, it may feel that the spell of desire has been broken. Like Beauty in the fairy tale "Beauty and the Beast," we cannot recognize our prince for the beast he seems to have become. The story of Benzai-ten can help us see past disillusionment into the true heart of love. Just as Beauty recognized the prince within the Beast, Benzai-ten's acceptance of her dragon-husband illustrates women's ability to recognize true love—even when it comes in unexpected packages.

One traditional tale about Benzai-ten tells how she acted as a go-between for a couple who had never met. While visiting a temple dedicated to Benzai-ten, a young man saw a piece of rice paper float from the air to rest at his feet. Written upon the delicate sheet was a love poem. The exquisite calligraphy suggested a feminine hand; immediately the young man knew he had to find the writer and marry her. But how could he do this? Deciding the goddess would take pity upon his mad quest, the young man resolved to pray at her shrine every night for a week.

At the end of his last evening at Benzai-ten's shrine, just as the dark sky had softened to morning's azure and the young man was about to leave, an elderly man walked in. He knotted one end of a scarlet thread around the young man's wrist, and placed the other as an offering into the temple fire. As the old man extinguished the flame, a young woman entered the temple. With skin as pale as the rice moon and hair as black as a starless night, she was as enchanting as that love poem had been.

"Benzai-ten has been moved by your prayers," the elderly man announced to the younger one. "Now come meet your bride." He explained that the beautiful woman had been the writer of the calligraphy that had intoxicated the young man. They were wed, blessed by the goddess.

The scarlet thread is a common motif in many Japanese folktales. It is believed to bind a couple destined to be together—the thread connecting them is as unbreakable as fate itself. Whether we are in a committed relationship or seek to be, many times it is not easy to recognize who is at the end of our scarlet thread. Instead, we see it tied to our beliefs of how things should be. The story of Benzai-ten can free us from these expectations.

HERA

Hera was honored as the goddess of marriage in ancient Greece. As ruler of this sacred institution, she was responsible for its protection. Her anger when the bonds of matrimony were not respected is perhaps as legendary as her difficult, tempestuous relationship with her husband Zeus, the powerful ruler of the Greek gods and goddesses.

To win Hera as his bride, Zeus courted her for three hundred years upon the island of Samos, the goddess's birthplace. Frustrated by his lack of success, he transformed himself into a cuckoo. Hera, charmed by the bird, allowed it into her lap, where Zeus immediately took back his natural form and seduced her. But marital happiness was not to be had: The god was as notoriously unfaithful to Hera as she was loyal to him. He had affairs with many women, including the mortal Danae and the divine Maia. Hera's anger at Zeus's infidelity was often expressed in the form of storms as violent as their domestic squabbling.

Sacred to Hera are the pomegranate and the lily—two potent symbols of feminine fertility seen in many cultures around the world—as well as oxen, trees, and mountains. Ancient rituals to Hera usually involved the use of these elements in some way or form.

FOR BETTER OR WORSE

As Hera Zygei or Hera the Joiner, Hera presided over marriage ceremonies and guarded the union itself. Wedding rituals are so rich in feminine symbolism that it is easy to recognize the influence of the Divine Feminine. They are perhaps one of the most significant and alchemic rituals that a woman can partake in. By participating in them, we cannot help but embody the goddess within ourselves.

The bride, dressed in her white gown, reminds us of the beauty of the moon, the most feminine of

celestial bodies. The honeymoon, referring to the lunar menstrual month, is the sweet moon of sensuality and love. Breaking the wine glass, a potent part of the Jewish wedding ceremony, represents the breaking of the maiden's hymen. The glass or cup shared by the newlywed couple symbolizes the womb, whose blood and nurturing waters bring new life into being.

The placing of a golden ring upon the third left finger derives from the medieval belief that a vein ran directly from that finger to the heart. It also suggests the act of intercourse. In pagan wedding ceremonies, also known as handfasts, the partners' hands are bound together with a knotted cord, the knot symbolizing eternity as well as the web of life that binds us together. This practice dates back to ancient Sumerian wedding rites.

Hera's wedding to Zeus was celebrated in Boeotia with a ritual utilizing symbols of the god and goddess. A piece of wood was carried to a shed in a cart drawn by oxen and set on fire. Oxen and trees were sacred to Hera; Zeus ruled over fire and lightning.

In many ways, this ancient ritual is tainted with traditional expectations of marriage. The male energy, symbolized by fire, devours the passive feminine—just as marriages were originally arranged for the sake of political or material alliances, the woman little more than a possession or slave.

Happily, the wedding ceremony has changed over time to reflect a more equitable relationship between husbands and wives, one based on affection. Though many couples may experience stormy unions, they no longer have to parallel the uneasy power division Hera shared with Zeus. Instead, Hera is remembered for her benign blessing of the ties that join woman and man in sacred matrimony.

XOCHIQUETZAL

The Aztec, a people who ruled over a vast empire in Mexico during the Middle Ages, believed in a flower goddess who they called Xochiquetzal. The goddess's sacred flower was the yellow marigold; her name meant "feather flower," referring to the marigold's many fine, feathery petals. One of the happiest of the Aztec deities, Xochiquetzal was also the goddess of dance, music, crafts, and love. Appropriately, her twin brother, Xochipilli, was honored as the god of pleasure.

Xochiquetzal lived on top of a mountain above the nine heavens. This flower-laden garden was populated by merry dwarves, dancing maidens, and musicians. The Aztec believed that anyone who was faithful to the goddess would spend eternity in her paradise when their earthly life had ended.

Xochiquetzal was married to the rain god Tlaloc, whose moisture helped her flowers to grow. Though many men fell in love with beautiful Xochiquetzal, she remained loyal to her husband for many years. But finally, the persistent and mischievous god Texcatlipoca won her affections from Tlaloc. Texcatlipoca loved Xochiquetzal so much that he sang of the goddess, "She seems to me a very queen, she is so lovely and so gay."

The Aztec also recounted a myth about a flood that destroyed all creatures except for Xochiquetzal and one mortal man. To repopulate the earth, they had many children, all of whom were born voiceless. But Xochiquetzal willed a dove to descend from the tree of heaven. After the dove gave each child a voice and a language, the children were scattered across the globe.

It was believed that all of the different races and languages in the world sprang from these children. With this story, the Aztec honored Xochiquetzal as the mother of the world.

UNDERSTANDING LOVE'S POWER

Rumored to be playful, beautiful, and extremely flirtatious, Xochiquetzal was desired by many. Many poems found upon Aztec manuscripts from this era praise this lovely goddess's gaiety, as well as her seductive, regal presence. Like the Greek goddess Persephone, Xochiquetzal was believed to be a young maiden; unlike innocent Persephone, Xochiquetzal was fully aware of the effect of her sexuality upon others. She often used these powers for her amusement and pleasure.

Some anthropologists believe that festivals to honor Xochiquetzal contained rituals that introduced the young to sexual pleasures in a safe environment. Today, young women especially need to approach the intoxication of love carefully. Perhaps an Aztec manuscript from the era of Xochiquetzal expresses this best. Within it, a parent advises his daughter to protect herself: "Understand that you are noble. See that you are very precious, even while you are still only a little lady. You are a turquoise . . . you are a descendant of noble lineage. . . ."

We would all do well to listen to this ancient father's timeless admonition. Like the recipient of this advice—like the goddess Xochiquetzal—we are all descendants of noble lineage. We are all divine, as is the gift of our love.

Benzai-ten

RELATED GODDESSES

Aine

The Irish goddess of love and light, Aine was honored on midsummer night. She was associated with both the sun and the moon. Some believe that during history's Middle Ages she was transmogrified into a fairy queen, who was mainly acknowledged in County Limerick.

Arundhati

In India, this goddess, whose name means "fidelity," is called upon in marriage ceremonies. Arundhati is the wife of Dharma and is often depicted upon a lotus leaf.

Blodeuwedd

The alluring flower goddess Blodeuwedd was first worshiped as a Celtic earth deity, who was married to the sun god Lleu. Later, her story was retold in *The Mabinogion,* a collection of Welsh myths. Within its pages, Blodeuwedd was magically created from flowers to wed Llew Llaw Gyffes, the son of Arianrhod. When she caused his death, the girl was transformed into an owl as punishment.

Erzulie

This Voodoo goddess of love is known for the luxury that she delights in. Erzulie is said to appear beautifully dressed and perfumed, with three wedding rings upon her hand; these bands represent her three husbands, the sky deity Dumballah, the ruler of the sea Agwe, and Ogoun, the warrior hero. She is also associated with the moon.

Fortuna Virginensis

Fortuna Virginensis is an aspect of Fortuna, the Roman goddess of luck. Newly married women honored her with the offering of their garments after their bridal night.

Fricka

Also known as Frigga, this Norse ruling goddess was married to the god Odin. Her domains included love, marriage, motherhood, and destiny. In the *Prose Edda,* a collection of myths from thirteenth century Iceland, Fricka was acknowledged as "foremost among the goddesses."

Ken

In Egyptian mythology, the goddess Ken bears attributes similar to Venus, the famed Roman goddess of love. She is usually depicted with a lion resting beneath her feet; lions were a potent symbol of power and divinity in ancient Egypt.

Lalita

In India, this youthful goddess of love and passion amuses herself by playing with the universe like a flirtatious woman plays with an enthralled lover. Appropriately, Lalita's name translates as "the amorous."

Tlazolteotl

Tlazolteotl was acknowledged in Aztec legend as a goddess of sexuality, as well as the patroness of midwives. Later, she was thought to purify her followers upon their death by devouring their misdeeds; in this function, she was known as the Filth Eater.

PART THREE

MOTHERHOOD

For the womb has dreams.
It is not as simple as the good earth.

ANAÏS NIN

Juno

MOTHER MOON, MOTHER EARTH, MOTHER NATURE, great mother of us all . . . The Divine Feminine has been invoked over the ages with these names and many others. It comes as little surprise that so many of the nurturing qualities associated with goddesses are the same as those required of mothers everywhere.

Each of the goddesses within this section offers us stories of motherhood. They express the giddying miracle of pregnancy and birth, the complexities of child rearing, and the difficulties experienced when a grown child leaves home.

Most mothers would agree that the patience and skill of a goddess is needed to successfully raise a child. Many might also agree that motherhood can be one of the more rewarding roles of the many offered to women in our lives. Whether we choose to give birth to a baby, adopt, or help another raise a child, few things are more goddess-like and all-encompassing than motherhood.

YEMANJA

Yemanja, the Santeria goddess of the ocean, is believed to be the daughter of the earth goddess Oddudua, and the sister and wife of the god Aganju. As the mother of the fourteen gods and goddesses who make up the pantheon, Yemanja occupies an exalted position in the Santeria religion.

Santeria developed during the nineteenth century from the Yoruba religion practiced by enslaved Africans who were brought to Cuba to work on sugarcane plantations. Since the Yoruba were not allowed to practice their native beliefs, they camouflaged their rituals with the symbols of the Roman Catholicism they were forced to observe; one example of this is the affinity of the goddess Yemanja to the Virgin Mary. By this practice, the Yoruba remained loyal to their *orishas,* or deities, and avoided detection and punishment. The Santeria religion spread from Cuba, where it originated, through the Caribbean to North and South America. It is still widely practiced today.

At some time in their lives, each practitioner of Santeria chooses one of the gods or goddesses to be their spiritual parent. Those who are the children of Yemanja try to please the goddess in many ways. Since seven is the number sacred to Yemanja, they wear seven silver bracelets on their arms. They also burn candles as blue as the ocean Yemanja rules. Beautiful blue and crystal beads, strung into necklaces as ethereal as iridescent moonlight upon the sea, adorn their necks.

THE WATERS OF LIFE

Since Yemanja is the powerful goddess of the waters, many honor her with the title of Holy Queen Sea. Appropriately, she is said to rule over every sea creature. She also owns all the riches of the ocean—pearls, oysters, coral reefs, and seashells. From time immemorial, seashells have been credited with mys-

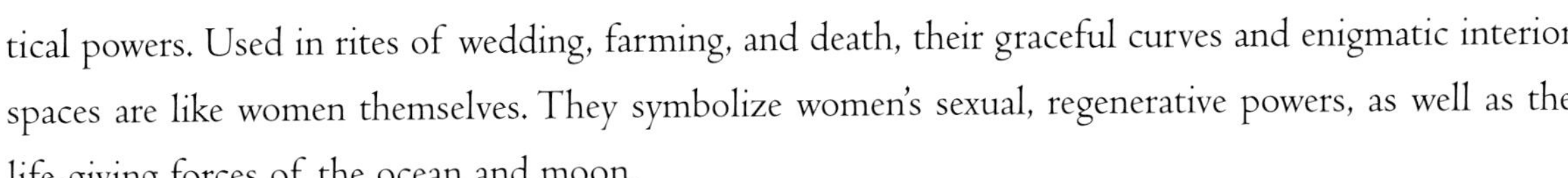

tical powers. Used in rites of wedding, farming, and death, their graceful curves and enigmatic interior spaces are like women themselves. They symbolize women's sexual, regenerative powers, as well as the life-giving forces of the ocean and moon.

Moon, sea, women—the eternal cycles of life—all fall under Yemanja's expansive domain. This graceful goddess is also believed to bring rain to nourish the earth.

The waters that nurture new life within a woman's womb are analogous to the life-giving ocean ruled by Yemanja. Appropriately, this goddess reigns over fertility and is revered as the great mother of all. Like the Virgin Mary with whom she is associated, Yemanja is often invoked by women who are having difficulty conceiving a child. For when a child is born of the waters, arriving like a beautiful pearl from an oyster shell, who can deny the power of Holy Queen Sea?

JUNO

The ancient Romans worshiped a supreme goddess they called Juno. Juno ruled over all aspects of Roman life with her consort, the god Jupiter. Besides being honored as the great mother, this goddess was also invoked as Optima Maxima, meaning "best and greatest" of the goddesses. In the goddess's form as Juno Moneta, Juno was believed to rule over money and administration. Thus, bright offerings of money would be left at the goddess's shrine to honor and win her favor. In Greece, Juno was associated with the ruling goddess Hera.

Juno was believed to watch and protect all women from their first to last breath. It is for this reason that Roman women called their souls *juno,* in honor of the goddess. As the patroness of marriage, Juno restored peace between quarreling couples; one of her temples was used as a sanctuary for women who needed shelter from cruel husbands. To this day, many people consider the month of June, named after the goddess, to be the most favorable time to marry.

The peacock is associated with Juno because the many eyes in its feathers are like the goddess's ever-open eyes as she watches over and protects women. As well, the richly colored plumes of the peacock were believed to be similar to Juno's beautiful robes. Because of this, Roman men and women carried *flabella,* ornate fans made out of peacock feathers, during the sacred rites of Juno.

MOTHER MOON

Originally considered a moon goddess, Juno was worshiped as the giver of light on the night of the full moon. From the earliest times, the moon was believed to magically influence the growth of crops, the

behavior of beast and human, and the ebb and flow of the sea. Round and full like a pregnant woman's womb, the moon symbolized the ability of women to bear children.

Juno, when honored as Juno Lucina, protected expectant mothers and helped their babies grow to be strong. The title "Lucina" related to the belief that moonlight made the child grow within the womb like a seed hidden deep in the earth; it also revealed the trust women placed in the goddess's ability to help their unborn child emerge healthy and whole from their bodies.

Though all aspects of women's lives were important to Juno, paramount was a woman's ability to conceive and give birth to children. Accordingly, all newborn children were said to be blessed and guarded by her. Juno was often invoked by young couples yearning for children, as well as by mothers laboring in childbirth. They believed the goddess would shield them from many dangers and illnesses. It is perhaps for this reason that Juno was also honored as the Preserver and Queen of Mothers.

Juno Lucina, Queen of Mothers, was honored every March first in a festival called the Matronalia. Women from all over journeyed to her great temple on the Esquiline in Rome. This was a time for women to join together and share stories of their experiences as matrons, mothers, and women. During this festival, they asked the goddess to bless their families—and themselves—for the coming year.

HAUMEA

Haumea, a Polynesian goddess, was credited with teaching women how to give birth by pushing their babies out from between their legs. Before this, folklore claims that children were cut from their wombs, extracted by knife like a pit from ripe fruit. Thanks to Haumea, women were able to forgo this dangerous life passage.

Haumea mated with the god Kane Milohai. Their numerous children included Hi'iaka, who taught the hula dance to the Hawaiians, and Pele, the tempestuous fire goddess associated with volcanoes. One myth claims that Pele was born from the goddess's armpit, suggesting the overwhelming fertility of Haumea—life was created from all of her body, not just her womb. In some ways, Pele reflected the mirror aspect of Haumea. Just as Haumea creates life, Pele destroys with fire. Haumea was also credited with giving birth to many fantastic creatures who populated the earth.

Also a goddess of vegetation, Haumea is honored as the mother of Hawaii. It is appropriate that a goddess so closely associated with fertility would be tied to this verdant island paradise.

CREATION'S SORCERESS

Women's ability to bring forth offspring from their bodies is perhaps the greatest magic known to humanity. The child remains mysteriously unseen within the womb, until it grows big enough to emerge into the world as a new existence. This creation of life is a divine power that only women possess.

Not surprisingly, the strength of Haumea's life-granting abilities caused some to identify her as a sorceress—a woman who uses magic for ill gains—instead of as a goddess. She was feared as a bringer of famine, and, if angered, was accused of joining forces with her daughter Pele to rage against humans who displeased her.

A story reflecting this belief relates how Haumea the sorceress was killed by Kaulu, a trickster figure in Polynesian culture, perhaps in response to fear over her myriad magical abilities. However, a goddess as powerful as Haumea could not be contained by death. She immediately resurrected herself as an alluring young woman. In this new incarnation, the goddess mated with her children and grandchildren, and gave birth to numerous offspring—creating life from her own death.

RENENET

After the long nurturance of pregnancy comes the experience of childbirth. During this vulnerable time, Egyptian mothers of antiquity invoked Renenet, their goddess of birth.

Renenet was responsible for creating the baby's desire to suckle mother's milk, essentially the same as granting it life. But perhaps most important, Renenet granted the child its *ren,* or soul name—the secret name that animated it outside the womb.

As the goddess of childbirth, Renenet was honored as the Goddess of the Double Granary. This title refers to the twin nurturing forces of milk and grain, both needed to raise a healthy child. The goddess was often depicted in art as a woman with the head of a lion or serpent; the Egyptians believed these animals had divine powers, like Renenet herself.

Renenet was believed to be accompanied by Meskhenet, a midwife goddess. The Goddess of the Double Granary was also associated with Shai, a deity of fortune who decreed what events a person's life would hold. Ancient Egyptians saw little difference between Renenet and Shai, suggesting a belief that the destiny of a person could not be separated from the circumstances of their birth.

NAMING THE BABY

After the baby is born, after the mother's last powerful push propels it toward its first breath, wonder and awe often set in. Who is this beautiful child, so wrinkled from womb water, so red with the blood of life?

Though most mothers choose their baby's name before birth, many times this important decision is not finalized until meeting the child outside the womb. Above all, the name of a child defines who he or she is. It is an expression of their divine energy.

In ancient times, Renenet, the goddess of new babies and soul names, was thought to help new mothers connect with their mysterious newcomer to learn his or her true name—the name that would reveal and protect the child's true nature. This *ren* could only be bestowed upon the child by its mother.

In addition to protecting the newborn baby from harm, the magical sound of this name held within its syllables the child's future. It also revealed the framework of the child's personality and place in the world. This special name was kept secret; for an enemy to discover it was an opportunity to gain power over the name-bearer, since the fortune of the child was set in the name.

In many ways, the choosing of the child's name bears similarities to the ritual of confirmation, as practiced in the Catholic Church. To connect with the special strengths of a particular saint, children add the saint's name to their own when they reach a certain age. In this way, the powers of Renenet, Goddess of the Double Granary, continue in the world today.

THE WAWALAK

The dramatic story of the Wawalak, a pair of sister Australian aboriginal goddesses, demonstrates the strength of mothers throughout time.

Before Europeans colonized Australia, over four hundred nomadic tribes inhabited the continent. Today, their numbers are much reduced, but these aboriginal peoples still believe that the world was created in a mythic past called "the dreamtime."

During the dreamtime, the gods and goddesses who were sleeping beneath the ground awoke and wandered over the earth. As they traveled, they created the landscape and living creatures, and taught them the art of survival. Once the world was completed, these divine ancestors went back to sleep in their underground abode.

Of all the aboriginal gods and goddesses, one of the most renowned is Yurlungur, who was also known as the Great Rainbow Serpent. Yurlungur created the precious rain, which brought life to the earth. Accordingly, she was honored as the Great Mother and Father. The myth of the Wawalak illustrates the power of these fertility goddesses against the Great Rainbow Serpent.

During the dreamtime, the Wawalak traveled from the south to the north with their two newborn babies. They set up camp next to the water hole of the Great Rainbow Serpent. Unaware that the water hole was sacred, the goddesses accidentally polluted the waters with blood from their womb after giving birth.

In angry response, the pool flooded and rains poured down upon the women and their infants. Water flowed from the hole, threatening to sweep them away. The Wawalak held their babies tightly and covered them with their bodies. They sang and sang to appease the Rainbow Serpent's anger. But the instant the sisters rested to gain breath, Yurlungur arose from the water hole and swallowed the goddesses with their babies whole.

 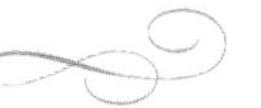

But not even a powerful deity like Yurlungur could undermine the mother strength of the Wawalak. Later, Yurlungur felt ashamed when she remembered what she had done. So she opened her great mouth to release the sister goddesses from their prison. Thus they and their children were reborn of the Rainbow Serpent.

MOTHER STRENGTH

Since then, the place where the Wawalak and their babies were reborn from the Great Rainbow Serpent has been a sacred spot for religious ceremonies. As both goddesses and mothers, the Wawalak symbolize the unending force of life in all women—a force that can never be suppressed.

The Kunapipi, an aboriginal cult, celebrate the miraculous rebirth of the Wawalak with an elaborate ritual incorporating dances that reenact their story. This fertility ceremony celebrates the return to the womb symbolized by the swallowing of the Wawalak, and the birth-giving powers of women. Two women are chosen to play the part of the Wawalak sisters and are painted with ochre, a bloodlike pigment. During this ritual, the women are ceremonially reborn from Yurlungur.

The Kunapipi also believe that in the beginning women knew every divine secret and owned all sacred objects and the special knowledge these items gave to their owners. Later, men stole them away to undermine women's powers.

For women who feel overwhelmed as they undergo the tests of motherhood, the story of the Wawalak reassures us that we possess all the wisdom we need within ourselves. All we need to do is allow it to emerge.

DEMETER

In the joy of creating new life, it is difficult to think of how the birth of a child begins its separation from its mother; each day as the child grows, it gains skills which will enable it to live on its own in time. The story of Demeter, the Greek goddess of the harvest, has offered consolation through the ages to mothers struggling with an empty nest.

Demeter's love for her daughter, Persephone, was so great that the two were inseparable. When Persephone was abducted by Pluto, god of the underworld, to become his bride, Demeter searched to the ends of the earth for her child. She even visited Hekate, goddess of the dark moon. She soon learned that Zeus had allowed Pluto to wed Persephone. At this news, grief and anger overwhelmed the goddess. So that the earth might reflect her sorrow, Demeter halted all plants from flowering and ripening.

For the first time ever, winter came and cloaked everything with snow. Humans began to starve from lack of food. Finally, to appease Demeter, Zeus agreed to allow Persephone to return to her mother, as long as she had not eaten while she was away. But Persephone had eaten: Six seeds of the pomegranate had passed her lips, this act symbolizing her acceptance of her husband. As a compromise, Persephone had to spend six months each year with Pluto, but was allowed to remain on earth with her mother for the remainder of the year. Upon her reunion with Persephone, Demeter allowed the earth to bloom again for their time together.

Not only does this myth explain the origin of the seasons, it offers hope to mothers who suffer the isolation of the empty nest. The winter of sadness and deprivation will pass. Spring will arrive again, if we are patient.

THE EMPTY NEST

Besides the Eleusinian mysteries (see page 35), the most important ritual associated with Demeter was the Thesmophoria. Called "the festival of sorrow" by the Boeotians, the Thesmophoria was celebrated by married women and mothers each October. As a reenactment of Demeter's grief over her separation from Persephone, this ritual of mourning and catharsis offered women a chance to express difficult feelings associated with motherhood and marriage. For many, it also allowed them the only chance they had all year to leave their homes and family responsibilities to spend time with other women.

The rituals of the Thesmophoria took place over three days. Like the Eleusinian mysteries, these rituals were enacted in secret. By participating in the Thesmophoria, women felt that Demeter would understand their sorrows and, consequently, they would be comforted by her acceptance. Each of the three days corresponded to the passage of the moon as it moves from waning to waxing in its cycle.

On the first day of the ritual, called either Kathodos ("downgoing") or Anodos ("upcoming"), women sacrificed pigs and tossed them into a serpent-filled hole, along with figures made of wheat and flour depicting humans and serpents. From that hole, they also drew up remains from the previous year's sacrifice and mixed them with seed corn. Some scholars believe that this sacred mixture was used by the women to create religious objects. It was on the second day, Nesteia ("fasting"), of the Thesmophoria that the women gave forth to the full range of their grief. As they fasted, they wept and expressed the pain so like what Demeter must have experienced. They also shared pomegranates, the fruit sacred to Persephone. The name of the final day, Kalligeneia ("fair-born"), suggests the catharsis that such a display of group emotion must have given these women.

For these women, the structure of the Thesmophoria offered a chance to work through the pain of separation while supported by a trusted group of women. It allowed them to honor their grief, and recognize its goddess-like divinity. Like Demeter herself, they journeyed through their sorrow toward a new life.

MAIA

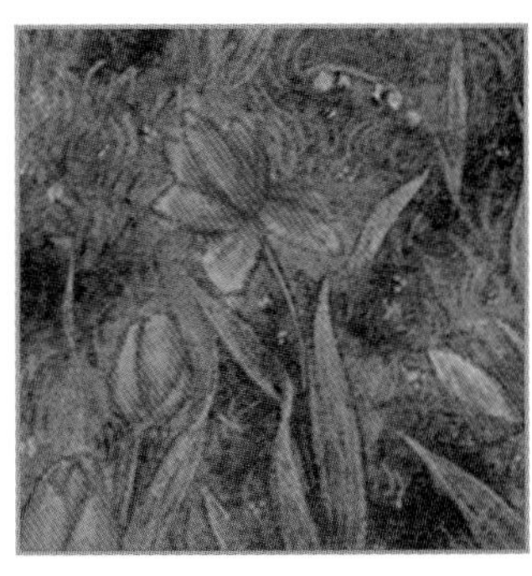

When we look into the night sky, we recognize the seven stars that make up the Pleiades, which is part of the constellation Taurus. The ancient Greeks believed that these stars were once the seven daughters of Atlas. Of these daughters, the goddess Maia was the eldest.

Atlas took part in an unsuccessful revolt led by the giants against the gods of Olympus. In punishment, he was forced to bear the world's weight on his shoulders. Maia and her sisters mourned their father's humiliation greatly—so much so that the gods turned them into doves to spare them further pain. The sisters then flew to the highest heaven, where they became the seven stars known as the Pleiades. Another story claims that the gods transformed the sisters to protect them from pursuit by the hunter Orion.

Maia is mainly remembered today as the goddess of spring and rebirth. Her name means "the maker." Like the earth itself, every spring this goddess is believed to make the lush green grass and fragrant flowers grow again.

She is also praised as the grandmother of magic because her son, the brilliant god Hermes, was the first to discover that mysterious art.

MOTHERING A CHILD, MOTHERING THE EARTH

Shy Maia was said to live alone in a cave on Mount Cyllene in Arcadia. Though she led a humble life, she did not escape notice: Zeus observed Maia's extraordinary beauty and came to her one night while his jealous wife slept. From this nocturnal encounter, Maia conceived Hermes, who was miraculously ready to be born by the time morning arrived.

Soon after the goddess gave birth to Hermes, Maia knew her son was a genius. While still a crawling baby, he created the first lyre by stretching strings across a tortoise shell, and the first panpipe from marsh reeds. Besides being the first magician, Hermes is credited with the invention of medicine, astrology, and letters. He was responsible for bringing the souls of the dead to the underworld as messenger to the gods and goddesses. Through this function Maia's son became known as a god of death—an interesting counterbalance to her role as bringer of life each spring.

People still celebrate Maia every year on the first of May, which is called May Day in honor of the goddess. Men and women rejoice over the return of spring by dancing circles around the maypole and by wearing vibrant green—the color of the reborn earth.

Demeter

RELATED GODDESSES

Abeona

Originally worshiped in ancient Rome as the goddess of departures, Abeona protects children as they leave their homes to enter the great world.

Ajysit

This birth goddess, worshiped by the Yakut in Siberia, was believed to relieve the pain of mothers in labor. She visited the family only during the birth of their child. Ajysit was also responsible for the new baby's soul.

Anuket

In ancient Egypt, Anuket was acknowledged as the benevolent Giver of Life; her name translates as "to embrace," or "embracer." This goddess was primarily associated with the nurturing waters of the Nile. She was honored during its annual flooding with an ecstatic festival of thanks.

Heqet

Like Anuket, Heqet was also associated with the Nile. This Egyptian fertility goddess is represented with the head of a frog, perhaps because the banks of the Nile are overrun with these amphibians after it floods. She ruled over childbirth; in honor of her life-giving properties, her servants were trained as midwives.

Kishijoten

In Japan, the goddess Kishijoten is acknowledged as a protector of children. Some also associate her with the arts practiced by geishas. Mothers ceremonially invoke her to watch over their infants and keep misfortune away.

Mut

Mut, whose name means "mother," was thought by the ancient Egyptians to help mothers give birth to children with sound bodies. She was honored as patroness of the city of Thebes, and often depicted in the form of a woman's body with a vulture head.

Rohzenitzn

This reindeer goddess, honored in Siberia, was believed to be responsible for the fate of newborn infants.

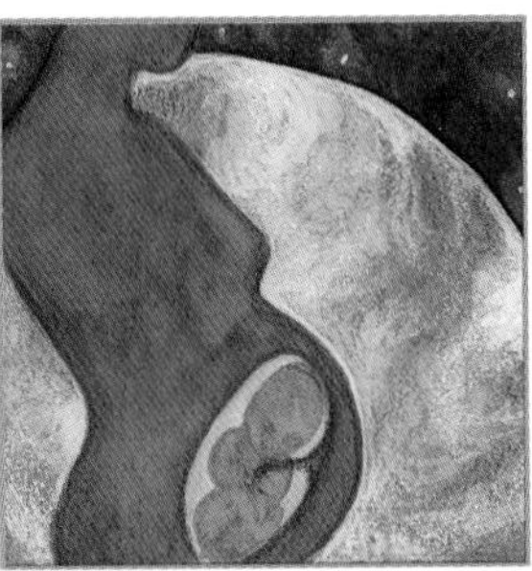

Sar-akka

In Scandinavia, this powerful Saami goddess helped open the womb for the laboring mother. She also created the fetal flesh grown within it. After the birth, Sar-akka was invoked in a ritual to predict the little one's future. She was also believed to have created the world.

Saule

Saule, a generous sun goddess, was honored in Lithuania. In addition to helping mothers with childbirth, Saule was also a goddess of weaving, spinning, and other household affairs.

PART FOUR

CREATIVITY

Bestower of intelligence and success,
O goddess, bestower of worldly enjoyment and liberation . . .

LAHLAKSHMI STOTRAM

Lakshmi

FROM TIME IMMEMORIAL, WOMEN HAVE HELD A special relationship with the creative spirit. When we give way to that connection, we are as powerful as any goddess. Our creativity is an unequivocable affirmation to the world of the divinity that illuminates us. For it is art that lifts our spirits, reminding us of our grand association with the universe that created us.

The goddesses offered in this section present many facets of feminine creativity, ranging from the refinements of civilization to the warmth of home; the aesthetics of art to the wisdom of knowledge. They show that the courage of our artistry can move ourselves, as well as others, toward transformation.

Whether we reveal our creativity through the medium of paint, words, music, or home, all acts of creativity are ultimately expressions of hope and beauty. They also reveal the face of the Divine Feminine.

BRIGIT

The fire of inspiration is a gift all writers and poets yearn to experience. Celtic people of long ago entreated the goddess Brigit for this divine spark that makes ideas take flight and become art. On the Scottish Isles, Brigit was often seen in the form of a beautiful white swan, as elusive as inspiration itself. Others believed that the goddess possessed an orchard of magical apple trees.

Wise Brigit was thought to take the form of a triple goddess, with each aspect of her divinity bearing a special function. As Brigit, goddess of poetry, poets asked her to take possession of their imaginations to bring forth words capable of moving people to tears and laughter. Brigit, the goddess of smithing, taught humans the important craft of forging iron, allowing them to create tools to aid their work; perhaps as a reflection of this, some believe her name translates as "the fiery arrow." Finally, Brigit, the goddess of healing, shared her knowledge of herbs to heal the ill.

Brigit was the daughter of Dagda, an earth god associated with life and death, as well as magic and art. With song from his divine harp, he was able to create the turn of the seasons.

The goddess Brigit proved to be so popular that she is still worshiped today as Saint Bridget. Unable to do away with her, the Catholic Church transformed her miraculous powers into miracles worthy of canonization.

THE FIRE OF INSPIRATION

Brigit's sacred holiday, the feast of Imbolg, is observed the first of February. It is a celebration that welcomes the return of light after the dark winter. It also marks the start of lambing season, and the new life that arrives with the start of spring. For this holiday, bards and poets were given special bells to tie to their walking sticks; perhaps these bells were a way of granting recognition to those who had received genius from the goddess.

Many rituals were performed at Imbolg to win the favor of Brigit for the coming year. In Scotland, on the night before Imbolg, a sheaf of oats would be dressed up and placed in a basket next to a thick wooden club. This basket, called Brigit's Bed, was laid in the hearth and allowed to burn by the women of the household. If an impression in the shape of the club was left in the hearth the next morning, it was believed that Brigit had chosen to bring good fortune to that home. People also attempted to prophesy by spreading ashes upon their hearth, later looking to see if the goddess had left her footprint within them.

To receive the inspiring wisdom of Brigit, many would hang a white wool cloth outside on the eve of Imbolg. The next morning, they fetched the cloth, believing it had absorbed the energy of the goddess. This sanctified cloth would be set aside in a special place, to be called into service when inspiration was required from Brigit, goddess of creativity.

SOPHIA

The goddess Sophia was considered the divine embodiment of female wisdom; her name translates literally as "wisdom" in Greek. In the ancient Near East, Sophia provided humans with the knowledge needed to create literature and the arts. Sophia symbolized the soul in its purest manifestation, often represented in art as having the form of a dove; the dove was also sacred to the Greek goddess Aphrodite.

Later history associated Sophia with the Holy Spirit in Gnosticism. Interestingly, Christianity depicted the Holy Spirit as a dove, imparting divine energy to its recipients.

POSSESSING KNOWLEDGE

Gnosticism—derived from *gnosis*, the Greek word for knowledge—grew alongside early Christianity. An important tenet of gnosticism held that knowledge could free humanity from the shackles of limitation; it enabled the divine spirit every person possessed to return to the One, the unknowable sacred source of creation. Some gnostic traditions claimed Sophia was the mother of Christ. Others associated her with the serpent in the Garden of Eden, who offered wisdom instead of temptation. Some accused Sophia of causing men to fall into confusion as they yearned for the One; one wonders if this was a way to decrease the power of a female deity.

Later, the Greek Orthodox church named her Saint Sophia, claiming her wisdom for their own; Saint Sophia was a virgin martyr. Hagia Sophia, also known as the Church of the Holy Wisdom, is one of the most beautiful examples of Byzantine architecture. It still stands in Istanbul, where the classical worlds of the East met the West. Its breathtaking mosaics and marble surfaces suggest the importance wielded by the goddess Sophia, even in her diluted form as Saint Sophia.

ATHENA

Athena, the goddess of wisdom, was one of the most powerful of the ancient Greek goddesses. She was the daughter of Zeus, the Greek ruling god, and his first wife, Metis, whose name meant "wisdom."

The unusual circumstances of Athena's birth foretold her great intelligence. Metis warned Zeus that the first son they produced would grow to be more powerful than Zeus himself. Zeus was so agitated by this news that when she became pregnant, he swallowed Metis and their unborn child whole. After this huge meal, the god had a terrible headache, which was relieved only when he split his head open with an axe. From the wound rushed forth Athena, fully grown and fully armored.

Instead of marrying, Athena chose to devote herself to wisdom and art, thus avoiding the romantic intrigues of the gods and goddesses. She came to be revered not only as the goddess of wisdom but also as the goddess of war. Skilled without equal in the art of battle, this goddess gave just protection to those in need of defense, especially to Achilles, the hero of *The Illiad.*

Athena's brilliance of reason was said to be as penetrating as her clear gray eyes. Her artistry in all crafts, especially weaving and pottery, was unrivaled. Only once was Athena's dominance challenged: Arachne, a mortal woman, invited her to a weaving contest. When Arachne lost, the goddess transformed her into the eternally spinning spider.

Often depicted with an owl, a symbol of enlightenment, and a serpent, a symbol of fertility, Athena is credited with the invention of the plow and the rake, which helped humans cultivate food. She also inspired architects to create elegant temples, many of which were strong enough to provide security in times of war.

Athena gave her name to Athens, the capital city of Greece. Poseidon, god of the seas, grew jealous of her popularity and proposed a contest: Whoever gave the most valuable gift to the Greeks would

become patron of the city. Poseidon gave a saltwater well. But Athena's gift of the olive tree provided shade from the hot sun, oil for lamps, and delicious olives to eat. From that time, all Athenian families have held the olive branch sacred as a symbol of Athena's generosity to them. It is also a universal symbol of peace.

THE WISE ARTISAN

A goddess of peace, and a goddess of art, too many still know only of wise Athena's skill at battle instead of her championship of the creative arts. It was for these powers as an artist—not as a warrior—that she was first valued throughout the ancient world of the Greek Isles.

What would our lives be like without the gifts of weaving, architecture, and pottery? Athena is the creator of all of these arts and many more. Worshiped as the mother of art, the goddess's form as Athena Ergane (or Athena Workerwoman) was the patroness of spinning and weaving—potent handicrafts associated with women's sacred work as the weavers of fate.

Each year in ancient Greece, to celebrate their own creativity as well as to honor Athena's, the females of Athens worked together to weave, sew, and embroider a new *peplos,* or woolen robe, for the statue of Athena housed in the Parthenon. This *peplos* incorporated scenes from Athena's myth and was woven of rich colors. It was begun nine months earlier at the Chalkeia, a celebration dedicated to Athena Ergane and Hephaestus, the god of metalwork and forging.

Today, many women associate Athena's wise creativity with career aspirations rather than artistic inspiration. While careers often allow room for the creative, it is important to express our artistry outside the workplace as well as within it. The story of Athena encourages us to pursue any latent creative talents we may possess.

FREYJA

In Norse mythology, gods and goddesses are divided into two groups, known as the Vanir and the Aesir. The peaceful Vanir grew food from the earth and were worshiped during the agricultural Bronze Age. Later, during the Iron Age, when human beings developed the first weapons and hunting tools, the combative Aesir were honored.

Not surprisingly, the Aesir brought war into the serene world of the Vanir. To settle this discord, the Vanir agreed to give the Aesir the goddess Freyja, the incomparably beautiful daughter of Njord, god of fair winds. In this way, Freyja became the link between the old world, before the invention of iron tools, and the new, where weapons were often used to create might over right. She can be seen as a mediator between peace and violence.

Freyja also presided over the living and the dead. As such, the goddess was responsible for the souls of half the warriors who perished in battle. After their death, these men were taken to Freyja's grand hall in Asgard, the home of the Aesir gods and goddesses. Their afterlife was filled with numerous joys and pleasures. The warriors were brought delicious food and drink by Freyja's graceful serving maidens. They listened to the goddess's favorite poems about brave deeds of honor, and favorite songs about love.

Despite the cheerful company of her warriors, Freyja was often sad. Freyja was married to Od, the god of ecstasy, but he vanished soon after the birth of their daughter, Noss, whose name means "delight." When Freyja missed her husband too much, she wept tears of gold. Sometimes she looked for Od, riding through the sky in her golden chariot drawn by two gray cats. At other times, she wore a falcon-skin cloak, which enabled her to fly through the air like a bird.

CREATING BEAUTY

Despite her duties on Asgard, Freyja was mainly honored as a goddess of beauty and love—forces more powerful than war and death. Just as Freyja's beauty settled the war between the Vanir and the Aesir, beauty has the ability to move all those who experience it—even the goddess herself. An example of this is illustrated in the famous story of Freyja and the Brisingamen.

The Brisingamen was the most beautiful necklace ever created. Smelt by four dwarves from the earth's purest gold, its exquisite curves shone like liquid fire conjured from the heart of the sun. As soon as Freyja saw the Brisingamen, she knew she had to have it at whatever cost; only she could do justice to its beauty. The goddess offered all the money she possessed. But the dwarves refused to part with it unless she would sleep with each of them—a fair exchange of beauty for beauty.

Freyja reluctantly agreed, though the dwarves did not please her in any way. But she quickly forgot her humiliation in the joy of owning the Brisingamen. It became her favorite possession; she was rarely seen without it upon her long, white neck.

When compared to the pragmatic needs of life, the creation of beauty is something society often views as unnecessary. But it is a powerful need—how empty our lives would be without beauty! The story of Freyja and the Brisingamen is an example of the power beauty can wield over even the most beautiful. Apparently it was well worth it: So stunning was this piece of jewelry that the Norse call the Milky Way "Freyja's necklace."

THE MUSES

Invoked by poets, artists, and musicians, these nine nymph-like goddesses presided over the arts and sciences in the world of the ancient Greeks. The Muses offered their supplicants the purest form of inspiration—literally infusing spirit into creative works to animate them.

The Muses were often worshiped with libations of milk, honey, or wine, which were poured upon the earth. They were especially honored in Boeotia, where the oldest city in Greece originated. Parnassus, a mountain that towered over the sacred site of Delphi, was considered the birthplace of the Muses; Apollo, the god of music and other arts, was also associated with Parnassus. Poets from Roman times believed that a sacred spring ran from Parnassus, bringing the gifts of the Muses to those fortunate to drink of it.

EXPANDING INSPIRATION

Though their parentage is uncertain, most stories hold that the Muses were the daughters of Mnemosyne, the goddess of memory, and Zeus. As such, the goddesses held a special place next to their divine father's throne, where they often sang songs in praise of the ruling god.

Originally there was only one Muse. Over time, they grew to number nine goddesses, suggesting the expansion of their powers. Each of the nine Muses concerned herself with an area of art. Calliope, the mother of Orpheus, was the most eloquent; she inspired epic poetry. Clio ruled over history, while Erato was usually depicted with a lyre. Other Muses included Euterpe (flute playing), Melpomene (tragedy), Polyhymnia (sacred music), Terpsichore (dance), Urania (astronomy), and Thalia (comedy).

The power of the Muses still exists today, though mainly in our language. When we are amused, we are reminded of the charms wielded by these graceful goddesses. Our ears are soothed by transforming music. Museums, latter-day shrines to the Muses, offer us inspiration and education.

MVSES

VESTA

The warmth of the hearth symbolizes the sun-like center of the home, and the loving emotions that bind us to it. The goddess Vesta was invoked as the procreative spirit of that place in ancient Rome. She was believed to be present in the hearth of each household, sanctifying each home with her warm, generous energy. This bountiful deity was known as Hestia to the ancient Greeks.

Vesta was experienced as a friendly presence who lived in the heart of a flame, rather than as a being with a physical body. A few pieces of art from this long-ago time depict her as a mysterious, veiled figure—more spirit than flesh and blood. Other art reveals Vesta as a regal woman, her generous figure completely covered by long robes and a head veil.

Vesta was a central figure in the Roman pantheon of gods and goddesses. Families would honor Vesta each day with an offering to their hearth. This offering was believed to bring continuing prosperity to the household. It also helped to create the perpetually renewing bonds of home, which hold people together in warm affection.

THE WARMTH OF HOME

Vesta, goddess of the hearth, shows us the importance of creating a home—a welcoming place where we belong; a haven that protects us from the harsher elements of the world. The creative skill of making a home deserves respect and honor. It is an art sacred to Vesta.

Today, Vesta is perhaps best known for her priestesses, the Vestal Virgins. These women, to whom the title "virgin" meant they had chosen to not marry rather than a lack of sexual activity, lived within her round temple. They were responsible for maintaining the goddess's eternal flame and sacred vessel.

Kept within this vessel were water, milk, and wine mixed with fruits and grains, perhaps to suggest the nourishing plenty of the earth. Vesta's flame represented the well-being of Rome; a priestess who allowed it to go out could be beaten as punishment for her mistake.

The Vestal Virgins honored Vesta and her sacred flame every June at the Vestalia. For this festival, Roman women brought sacrifices of baked goods to her temple-home, while the Vestal Virgins offered cakes of salt cooked upon the temple's hearth. Vesta's flame was rebuilt by the Romans every March first for the year.

Today, homes have replaced religious institutions as havens of warmth. Accordingly, many of our domestic arts have replaced the ceremonies of Vesta. To comfort ourselves, we bake cookies on cold winter days, or huddle around the warmth of a fireplace. We build campfires upon beaches at night, to create light where there was once darkness. In these simple but reassuring acts, remnants of Vesta's ancient rites can still be found.

LAKSHMI

Lakshmi is treasured in India as the goddess of prosperity and beauty. She is believed to represent all that is wonderfully feminine, while her consort, Vishnu, the conqueror of darkness, represents all that is masculine. Many delicately detailed paintings from India show Lakshmi and Vishnu riding on the back of Garuda, the king of birds, as they fly across the land.

According to Indian mythology, the goddess Lakshmi was created from the Ocean of Milk. Vishnu churned the Ocean of Milk for Indra, king of the gods, to make a magic potion that would bestow eternal life. As Vishnu churned the ocean, many wonderful things came out of it, including a wish-granting cow, an elephant, and a handsome white horse. But most precious of all was beautiful Lakshmi.

As Lakshmi rose out of the Ocean of Milk upon her lotus flower throne, elephants bathed her with water poured from golden vessels. The ocean dressed the goddess in a wreath of unfading lotuses; jewels as bright as stars wrapped themselves around her plump, graceful arms and neck. All who looked upon Lakshmi knew instant happiness.

The goddess immediately announced that her place was next to Vishnu's heart. Fortunately, Vishnu agreed. Lakshmi married Vishnu, and they soon had a son named Kama. Kama came to be considered the god of romantic love; in many paintings, he looks similar to cherubs depicted on greeting cards for Valentine's Day. These three deities represent the abundant promise of wealth the world can offer us—if we choose to accept its blessings.

WORLDLY PROSPERITY

Creating prosperity can be as creative an act as any artistic endeavor. Lakshmi, the goddess of abundance, shows us that wealth can be divinely inspired. As the sacred manifestation of all forms of prosperity, she is perhaps the most popular of the Hindu gods and goddesses. Lakshmi is often depicted upon coins as bright as the fortune she offers her devotees.

Lakshmi is believed to be attracted to sparkling jewels, which are like the riches she bestows. Statues of the goddess show her wearing gold and other precious gems, and surrounded by verdant lotuses. Some people believe that she lives in the sky with the most beautiful jewels of all, the stars.

To honor Lakshmi's powers, the festival of Divali is celebrated every November on the night of the new moon—when the stars are at their brightest. Some believe that this is the day that Lakshmi and Vishnu were married. The goddesses Sarasvati and Kali are also acknowledged during this sacred and joyful celebration.

As part of the preparations for Divali, households across the land are made shining and clean; since Lakshmi loves shiny, glittery things, it is thought that the more sparkling the home, the more likely she will visit it with blessings. Tiny clay lanterns, brilliant with light, line roofs, doorways, and window ledges. Families hope that these lanterns will attract the goddess's observant eye to their homes, so that Lakshmi, goddess of prosperity, will honor them for the coming year.

SARASVATI

Sarasvati, the Hindu goddess of all knowledge, is held in special esteem in India by students, writers, and musicians. Extraordinarily beautiful and graceful, Sarasvati is easily recognizable by her dazzling white skin and brilliant clothing.

One myth tells how Sarasvati and her consort, Brahma, were born from a golden egg that emerged from the sea. They then created all of the knowledge and all of the creatures in the world. Many consider Sarasvati the mother of life since it was her divine energy, united with the awareness of Brahma, which brought everything into being.

Pictures of Sarasvati show her seated upon a lotus-blossom throne, accompanied by a white swan. The swan is believed to be able to separate milk from water—an act that shows the ability to discriminate between actions that are good and those that are insincere. The goddess is usually depicted with four arms, symbolizing her powers' range over the earth's four directions. In one of her hands, she holds a book, representing education; in the other hand, a strand of beads, indicating spiritual knowledge. With her remaining arms, she holds a *vina*, an Indian lute, representing the art of music.

Sarasvati's grace and beauty are reflected in her name, which translates as "the flowing one"; this title refers to her dual role as a river goddess. In India, the pure, flowing waters of rivers suggest the purifying and nurturing waters of life; they are regarded as sacred. Sarasvati shares her name with a river that flows down from the Himalayan mountains to join the Ganges River. However, she is mainly honored as the embodiment of wisdom.

Along with the goddess Lakshmi, Sarasvati is especially worshiped during the autumnal festival of Divali.

THE WORD AND ITS SONG

Beautiful Sarasvati, as dazzling white as the swans that circle her lotus-blossom throne, is invoked by scholars yearning for her divine intelligence. Sarasvati's pure white form is said to be as brilliant as the light of knowledge. She is able to banish all forms of ignorance, bringing education to anyone wise enough to desire her enlightening presence.

As the personification of knowledge and education, all of the refinements of civilization fall under the goddess's wide-reaching domain. Sarasvati is credited with creating the fruits of civilization: the Sanskrit alphabet, the arts, mathematics, music, and magic.

This wise goddess is actively worshiped in many areas of Hindu life. University students perform ceremonies to honor her before examinations. Film directors invoke her help before beginning production on a new film. Musicians praise her with song; the music of the *vina* is especially sacred to Sarasvati.

Sarasvati is a well-loved goddess to this day. She is often honored with a traditional prayer, which invokes her luminosity:

O goddess Sarasvati, white as snow or the moon or the kunda flowers,
clothed in white garments, holding a magnificent vina,
seated on a white lotus and ever gloried . . .
Protect us from all forms of ignorance.

RHIANNON

In England, there is a huge impression of a horse carved in the chalk on the side of a Berkshire hill. This enormous white carving, dating from the first century BCE, suggests the importance of the horse to people of that time. Horses were used for traveling, plowing fields, and transporting heavy loads. Their strength made it possible for humans to support themselves from the land.

Like this horse carved within the earth, the British horse goddess Rhiannon was said to appear to her followers riding an unearthly white horse. Dressed in royal robes of gold, Rhiannon was always accompanied by three birds from the Happy Otherworld, where gods and goddesses live in eternal happiness. The magical song of these birds could lull the living to death, restore the dead to life, and heal all sadness and pain. The beauty of their song suggests the otherworldly beauty of this goddess.

Rhiannon's name is derived from *rigantona*, which means "great queen goddess." In an earlier period, Rhiannon was known as Epona. Many statues have been found of Epona, most of which depict her with a mare on one side and a bundle of grain on the other, symbolizing her connection to the harvest. Other statues depict a mare, foal, and goddess. They represent the goddess's ability to create food to sustain life.

CREATIVE CHANGE

Like the supernatural white horse Rhiannon rides, the goddess symbolizes the unceasing force of movement, which pulls all of life with it. This divine function is also suggested by a story from *The Mabinogion*,

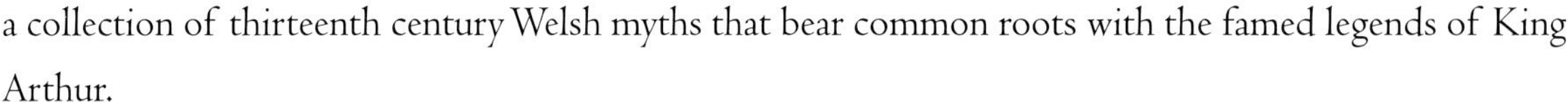

a collection of thirteenth century Welsh myths that bear common roots with the famed legends of King Arthur.

In *The Mabinogion,* Rhiannon appeared as an unattainable enchantress dressed in rich gold. Pwyll, the prince of Dyfed, fell in love with the goddess after spying her on her white horse. Pwyll guessed from her ethereal beauty that she was of divine origin, but he was undaunted. Determined to catch up to her, he rode his horse as fast as he could. But no matter how fast he rode—or how slowly Rhiannon appeared to ride—he was unable to reach her.

This went on for three days. Finally, the humbled prince called to the goddess to wait for him, which she did. When he asked, "Why didn't you stop earlier?" Rhiannon simply replied, "Why didn't you ask me?" And so Rhiannon accepted Pwyll as her consort. The couple lived together for many years, experiencing many trials and triumphs.

The story of Rhiannon and Pwyll suggests that the ability to create change is always within our reach. Sometimes all we need to do is state our desires—if we are intent enough, transformation is possible.

Athena

RELATED GODDESSES

ANNAPURNA

Many Hindus believe that this generous goddess helps create food to nourish the world. Often honored at harvest festivals, Annapurna is depicted in statues and paintings as sitting upon a grand throne, offering food to a small child.

BERCHTA

Berchta, the German goddess who spins the thread of destiny, is said to wear a mantle of snow upon her shoulders. She also presides over household affairs.

DANU

Honored in ancient Ireland as the greatest and wisest of all Celtic goddesses, Danu is considered to be the mother of the deities. She provides her followers with prosperity and knowledge.

GLISPA

The Navajo of the southwestern United States pay homage to this mysterious goddess, who brought them the sacred beauty chant. Glispa taught them the ways of music and healing, thus imbuing them with the powers of the shamans.

HALTIA

Haltia was believed to rule over houses among the Baltic Finns. This benevolent goddess was thought to be a part of the actual structure of the home, bringing good luck to its inhabitants.

HUCHI-FUCHI

In Japan, Huchi-Fuchi is the goddess of the hearth. Her fire is responsible for the creation of food, and the warming of the home.

IX CHEBEL YAX

Ix Chebel Yax was honored by the Mayans as an educator who taught women the arts of weaving, basket making, and other important crafts. She was believed to be the daughter of the moon.

ZHINU

This Chinese goddess is the patroness of weaving. Zhinu is responsible for making the grand robes worn by the Heavenly Emperor and his family. She is also associated with the stars.

PART FIVE

STRENGTH

A roof of cedar branches, pine pillows, bamboo blinds,
If only these could screen me from this world of sorrow.

LADY NIJO

Kuan Yin

WHILE THE WORLD IS NOT A VALE OF TEARS, THERE ARE TIMES when it seems more so than others. As strong as we may be, these are the times we need a special power—the potent strength of the Divine Feminine.

The goddess myths presented in this section express the strengths carried in women's souls, as well as those contained within our glorious bodies. They show us how to deal with the shadows contained within our hearts, bringing hope to difficult situations that may seem overwhelming.

For better or for worse, life encompasses all experiences, whether they be joyful or formidable. And so do these goddesses and their stories.

OYA

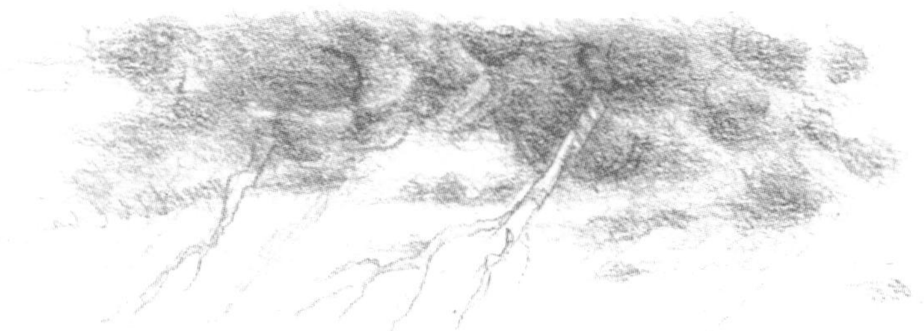

In Nigeria, the Yoruba people believe that the Niger River is ruled by a powerful goddess named Oya. When Oya is happy, the river flows smoothly, bringing clear water to nurture those who depend on it. But when she is angry, the river overflows or runs dry.

Oya is also responsible for sending storm winds to warn humans of the approach of her husband, the thunder god Shango. The divine couple live in a magnificent copper palace in the sky, from which they observe the Yoruba. Those who displease Oya and Shango are certain to receive visits from them in the forms of fire, violent storms, lightning, and flooding rivers.

One story relates that Oya was originally an antelope and was able to take off her skin at will, much like a coat. In the form of a mortal woman, she would go to the marketplace to spend time among humans. It was there that the thunder god Shango first saw Oya. He immediately lost his heart to her, and, to gain her hand in marriage, he hid her antelope skin. It did not take long for wise Oya to find out where her future husband had placed the skin. But Shango humbly begged her forgiveness and, in apology, offered her *akara*, her favorite bean cakes. Delighted, the goddess agreed to stay with Shango, and help him fight his battles against those who angered him.

To please Oya, many Yoruba wear decorative strands of long, maroon beads around their necks. Statues depict her wearing a headdress decorated with copper nails, which looks like Shango's thunder axe.

A popular goddess, Oya is actively worshiped to this day.

THE POWER OF WORDS

The wind that heaves trees from their roots and tears roofs from homes is also the wind we use to speak. This wind, produced by our living breath, creates the words we can use to empower ourselves. Yet, many times we find ourselves unable to speak when we most need to. The words that can aid us most do not come to our lips, or we are unable to say them because of our fears and insecurities.

Oya is often invoked by Yoruba women for help to gain the right words, which will erase conflicts and gain power. Valued for her charming but penetrating language, many consider the goddess a patroness of feminine leadership; her gift for eloquence helps women learn to speak with wisdom and confidence. With these skills, we can gain authority over any situation.

Oya is a goddess to be approached with great respect. In Nigeria, shrines to her are set into a corner of a home. The altars are often molded of packed earth, while a covered clay pot is used as a centerpiece. Arranged around it are magical amulets and objects: Copper coins symbolize the copper palace she shares with Shango; a sword represents Oya's power of incisive speech; strings of red, orange, or brown glass beads, buffalo horns, and locust pods also symbolize the goddess. Finally, small dishes of her favorite foods, eggplant and *akara,* are offered to please Oya, goddess of the winds.

KUAN YIN

Kuan Yin is one of the most beloved deities of China, and is considered to act as a guardian angel to humans. She is said to personify *karuna,* the principle of boundless compassion and kindness.

Before she became a goddess, Kuan Yin was the youngest of three daughters of a wealthy, cruel father. When she saw her father force her sisters to marry unkind but rich husbands, Kuan Yin asked instead to enter a temple for a life of contemplation and good works. Her father agreed, but secretly ordered the temple residents to give Kuan Yin the hardest chores to discourage her.

Kuan Yin had so much to do that, after toiling all day, she had to work all night while others slept. But the animals who lived near the temple witnessed Kuan Yin's hardships and decided to help her. The tigers gathered wood for the fire. The snakes brought water to the temple. The birds collected vegetables from the garden, while the spirit of fire cooked food for everyone.

News of these miracles spread from the girl's lonely temple and reached her father's ears. In a fury, he set fire to the temple. But Kuan Yin put out the fire with her hands without suffering one burn. Finally, her father gave orders for her to be killed for disobedience.

After her death, Kuan Yin was brought to heaven, where her compassionate heart earned her an eternity of bliss. But as she reached heaven's gates, the girl heard a cry from below. It was someone suffering upon the earth—someone in need of her help. Then and there she vowed never to leave humanity until every last person was free from woe.

For this promise, Kuan Yin was transformed into a goddess. Many people believe that she is still among us, looking after the many humans in need of her care.

MOTHER OF HEALING

Mother of mercy, mother of compassion and healing—all these honorifics describe Kuan Yin. Today this treasured goddess is widely worshiped by Taoists and Buddhists. She is believed to heal those sick in heart and body. She pays special attention to mothers and children in distress, and even seafarers in storms.

Too often in life, we are overwhelmed by troubles. Sorrow encompasses us, and there is only so much we can do. For those beset by worries or illness, merciful Kuan Yin is a wonderful goddess to invoke. Chinese families often place a small statue of Kuan Yin in a quiet spot in their homes. Many of these figures show the goddess gowned in white and seated upon a lotus throne, symbolizing enlightenment, and holding a small child. Others depict her pouring a stream of pure water, suggesting the waters of life, while holding a rice sheaf to offer nourishing strength. At these intimate shrines, flowers, fruit, or incense are placed as offerings.

Many people believe that even to say the goddess's name will bring protection and relief to those in need of her help. Others choose to go on pilgrimages to the goddess's temple on the mountain of Miao Feng Shan, which is set upon a faraway island. As they pray, they shake rattles and other noisemakers to attract the notice of Kuan Yin, goddess of mercy.

ISIS

From before 3000 BCE to the second century CE, Isis was worshiped in Egypt as the great mother goddess of the universe. Isis took care of everything to do with moisture. She was present every day at sunrise, and at the time of the new and full moon. Her milk nourished all living beings; her traditional headdress of a sun disk between two cow horns suggests these duties. Isis looked after the affairs of the day, while her sister, Nephthys, took care of the night. She also had two brothers, Osiris and Set. Osiris was responsible for the soil, and Set ruled the barren desert and the sea.

When the siblings were old enough, the sun god Ra married Isis to Osiris, and Set to Nephthys. Isis and Osiris were blissful in their love. They lived in such joyful harmony that all were moved by its beauty. Their days were spent nourishing the world—Isis's powers combined with Osiris's brought forth abundant food from the rich Egyptian soil and the fertile Nile. Their nights were blissful with love; no moon or star could outshine their passion.

Everyone adored Isis and Osiris—everyone except Set, their jealous brother. To bring an end to their idyllic rule, Set murdered Osiris and placed his body in a coffin. In time, a great tree grew around it.

Isis searched everywhere for her lost husband. When she finally found him within the tree, she retrieved Osiris. But Set stole Osiris's body away from her. To prevent Isis from being reunited with her beloved, Set cut Osiris into fourteen pieces and scattered them all over Egypt.

Undeterred, Isis turned herself into a bird and flew up and down the Nile, gathering each piece of Osiris. When she put them next to one another, she joined them with wax. She found that only Osiris's phallus was missing; this Isis formed of gold and wax. Then, using the power of her magic and of her love, Isis brought Osiris briefly back to life to conceive a child with him. That child, the falcon-headed god Horus, grew and thrived. In time, he brought vengeance upon Set for the murder of Osiris.

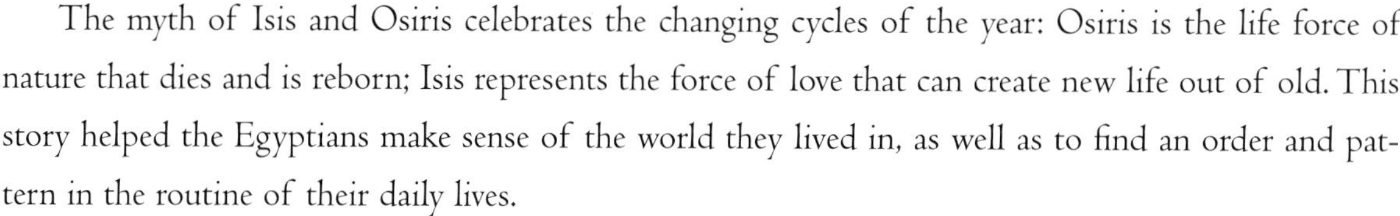

The myth of Isis and Osiris celebrates the changing cycles of the year: Osiris is the life force of nature that dies and is reborn; Isis represents the force of love that can create new life out of old. This story helped the Egyptians make sense of the world they lived in, as well as to find an order and pattern in the routine of their daily lives.

EASING HEARTBREAK

Gifted, magnificent Isis illustrates the strength of a woman who loves, and the transformative powers of her heartbreak. When heartbreak is not fully acknowledged, it spills into other parts of life, and paints it with sorrow. The suffering of Isis as she searched for Osiris up and down the Nile suggests the somber journey many women undergo to confront our pain and transform it.

In ancient Egypt, the myth of Isis and Osiris was reenacted each year in a great ritual of formal mourning. This ceremony was one of their most important religious rites. It allowed participants to experience the painful emotions of the goddess as she searched for and mourned her husband-brother. They also felt her joy at Osiris's rebirth in the form of Horus, their son. In the great Egyptian Book of the Dead, Isis is identified as the giver of nourishment and life to the dead. Just as she judged Set for his misdeeds, she also judges those who have passed on to the other side.

The powerful story of Isis continues to offer strength to women who are heartbroken from the loss of their beloved. It shows how we can create hope out of loss—like Isis's mystical resurrection of Osiris.

ARTEMIS

Artemis, the Greek goddess of hunting and the moon, reveals the physical strength and self-reliance of women everywhere. The moon, which tradition connects with the night, wild beasts, and women's bodies, suggests the vast compass of Artemis's mysterious realm. As a symbol of her sovereignty, Artemis wore a crown shaped like the crescent moon upon her brow; this headdress's shape also symbolizes animal horns. She was associated with the harvest moon and the winter solstice.

Artemis was honored as Diana in ancient Rome, and was praised for her strength and athletic grace; her skill as a huntress was unsurpassed. Hunting was especially important to humans at this time, because they relied on meat as a main source of nourishment, especially in winter when crops had finished for the year.

Independent and wild, Diana chose to join her life with no man. Instead, she lived unencumbered in the woods, her only companions a loyal band of nymphs and untamed animals. Those who did not respect the goddess's wishes met terrible deaths. One man, Acteon, so desired her that he disguised himself in a deer skin and antlers, then hid behind an oak tree to spy on her while she bathed. The goddess was not fooled, and in a fury, allowed her hunting dogs to tear him to pieces.

Some people believe that this legend describes a hunting ritual performed at the beginning of winter to ensure there will be food, rather than a warning about the hot temper of an angry goddess. Acteon symbolizes the stag that men hoped they would find in the forests. They prayed to Diana to help their hunting dogs to catch the stags, just as Diana's dogs caught the unlucky Acteon.

Oak groves and freshwater springs were especially favored by the goddess; many of her temples were located within them. But Artemis's most famed shrine was in Ephsus. There, a great statue of the goddess depicted her as many-breasted, honoring her ability to nourish all creatures—like the earth itself.

WOMEN'S STRENGTH

The story of Artemis is a celebration of women's physical strengths and women's friendships. Her rituals celebrated these qualities as well. Many of them encouraged girls and women to join together and dance wildly in the light of the full moon.

The Brauronia was one of the more important rituals to honor Artemis. To apologize to the goddess for the accidental slaying of a bear cub by a young girl, Athenian girls danced the *arkteuein*. This dance, whose name translates as "to act the bear," is self-explanatory: By dancing like a bear, young girls were allowed to let their inner wildness loose, and express their strength and athleticism.

To please the goddess, one cult devoted to Artemis encouraged her followers to let their teenage daughters live like bear cubs. These girls lived in the woods, unworried about appearance or manners. This gave them the chance to sow their oats before rejoining the world as women ready for marriage.

Worship of Artemis, goddess of hunting and the moon, extended across Europe. She was still believed to rule the wild forests until the Middle Ages. At that time, many people forgot that she was a goddess, and called her queen of the witches instead. They had forgotten that she symbolized the earth's ability to provide for all of its creatures—even in the harshest, coldest winters.

PELE

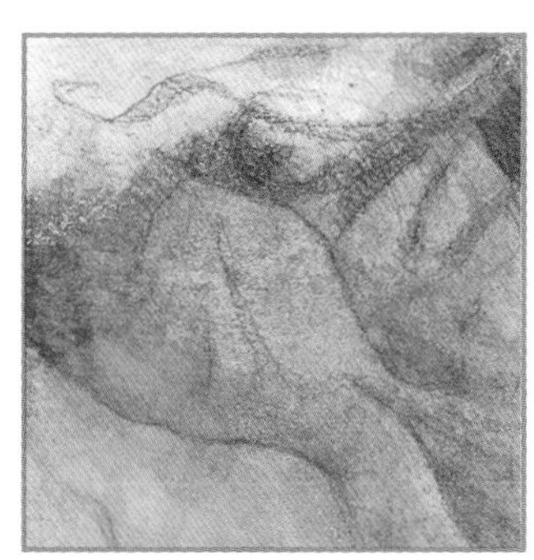

In the Hawaiian islands, where there are many volcanoes, people believe in a tempestuous goddess named Pele. Pele rules over all kinds of fire, but especially over the lava that flows from erupting volcanoes. The finest strands of molten lava are called "Pele's hair."

Everyday life would be harsh without fire to cook food or to heat homes in winter. But humans also live in fear of fire devastating their homes and forests. Like fire itself, Pele has the power to destroy as well as to create. If she is pleased by the islanders' prayers, she will generously halt the flow of hot lava aimed toward a village; if angered, she will turn people and animals to stone. Hawaiians also believe that earthquakes are caused by an angry stomp of Pele's foot.

One story claims that Pele was created by the heat of the earth, like lava from a volcano. Surprisingly, her first home was in the sea with Hi'iaka, her sea goddess sister, but she grew angry with Pele and drove her away. Pele wandered across the sea for a time; then she came to Hawaii. She is thought to have settled there in Mount Kilauea, one of the most active volcanoes in the world. The smaller lava formations found around the volcano are called "Pele's tears": Local legend says that ill fortune will visit those foolish enough to steal one of these pebbles from her realm.

Famed for her passionate love affairs as well as her temper, Pele often appears to her worshipers in the guise of a woman as beautiful as the moon. Others say she looks like a terrible hag, with brown flesh as crumpled as coarse lava. Whichever way the goddess chooses to present herself, all agree about her fiery temperament—and her ability to destroy as well as create.

THE PASSION OF ANGER

The passion of anger has an urgency that can help us better our lives. Pele's ability to present herself as either a wrinkled hag or a seductive woman suggests the inner turmoil that rage can create within women. It reveals the ugliness and discomfort that women often feel when angered, along with the empowerment that anger can make possible. Pele's story offers an antidote to these beliefs. She tells us that our anger is not only worthy, it is divine.

Simmering, erupting, boiling over, consuming—the language of fire is surprisingly similar to the language we use to describe anger and passion. Like lava from a volcano, these emotions have the capacity to annihilate when unchecked, as evidenced in the following story about Pele.

Hawaiians believe that to amuse herself, Pele sometimes visits them. In her incarnation as an alluring goddess, she is described by those who have seen her as the most beautiful woman on earth, with a back as straight as a cliff and round breasts. Her royal bearing and great charm make her irresistible. During one of these visits, Prince Lohiau, the chief of the island of Kaua'i, fell deeply in love with Pele. Unaware that the object of his affection was the divine goddess of fire, the prince insisted that they marry immediately. Since Pele loved him also, she agreed.

Three days after the wedding, Pele left her new husband to arrange her affairs, promising to return to him as quickly as she could. But divine time differs from human time, and she took too long: Prince Lohiau, thinking she had abandoned him, died of a broken heart. His encounter with the goddess had been as destructive as fire from the heart of a volcano.

THE ZORYA

In myths all over the world, there have always been trinities of goddesses who are believed to bear responsibility for the earth's well-being. Usually these three goddesses also symbolize the three ages of women—maiden, mother, and crone, or post-menopausal woman. Similar to the phases of the moon, the universal presence of these triple goddesses suggest the strength and authority of the Divine Feminine everywhere.

The ancient Greeks believed in three goddesses they called the Fates. These mysterious beings were said to write the world's future, which mere humans must wait to see unfold. In Scandinavian mythology, the three Norns wove the thread of life, which, if broken, would bring about the end of the world. The Morrigan, a trio of Irish warrior goddesses, were associated with the moon and had similar powers.

In Russian folklore, the Zorya are another trinity of sister goddesses. The three Zorya represent and are named after different times of the day. The first goddess is called Morning Star, or Utrennyaya; the second Evening Star, or Vechernyaya; and the third Midnight, or Zorya. They are also known as the Auroras.

PROTECTING LIGHT AND LIFE

The Zorya are attendants of Dazbog, the sun god who rides through the sky on his horse every day, bringing light and warmth to the earth. Some say Dazbog fathered the Zorya. He returns each evening to a magical isle ruled by the Zorya.

When Dazbog is ready to leave the isle at daybreak, Morning Star opens the gates of heaven to let him out. Since the sun god sets out in the morning and gradually grows older during the day, by night-

fall he is an old man. This is when he returns to the Zorya's magical isle, where Evening Star closes the gates behind him. During the night, the sun god is reborn as a new baby, ready to repeat the cycle the following morning.

As well as attending to the sun god, without whose light all living things would perish, the Zorya are considered guardians of the universe. As such, the goddesses are responsible for guarding a terrible doomsday hound, which is chained to the constellation of Ursa Minor, or Little Bear. Just as night devours the day, Russians believe that the hound yearns to devour the little bear. One legend states that if ever this chain were to break, the end of the world would be at hand.

Bringers of light, protectresses of the universe—these stories reveal the importance of the Zorya in ensuring the continuity of life on earth.

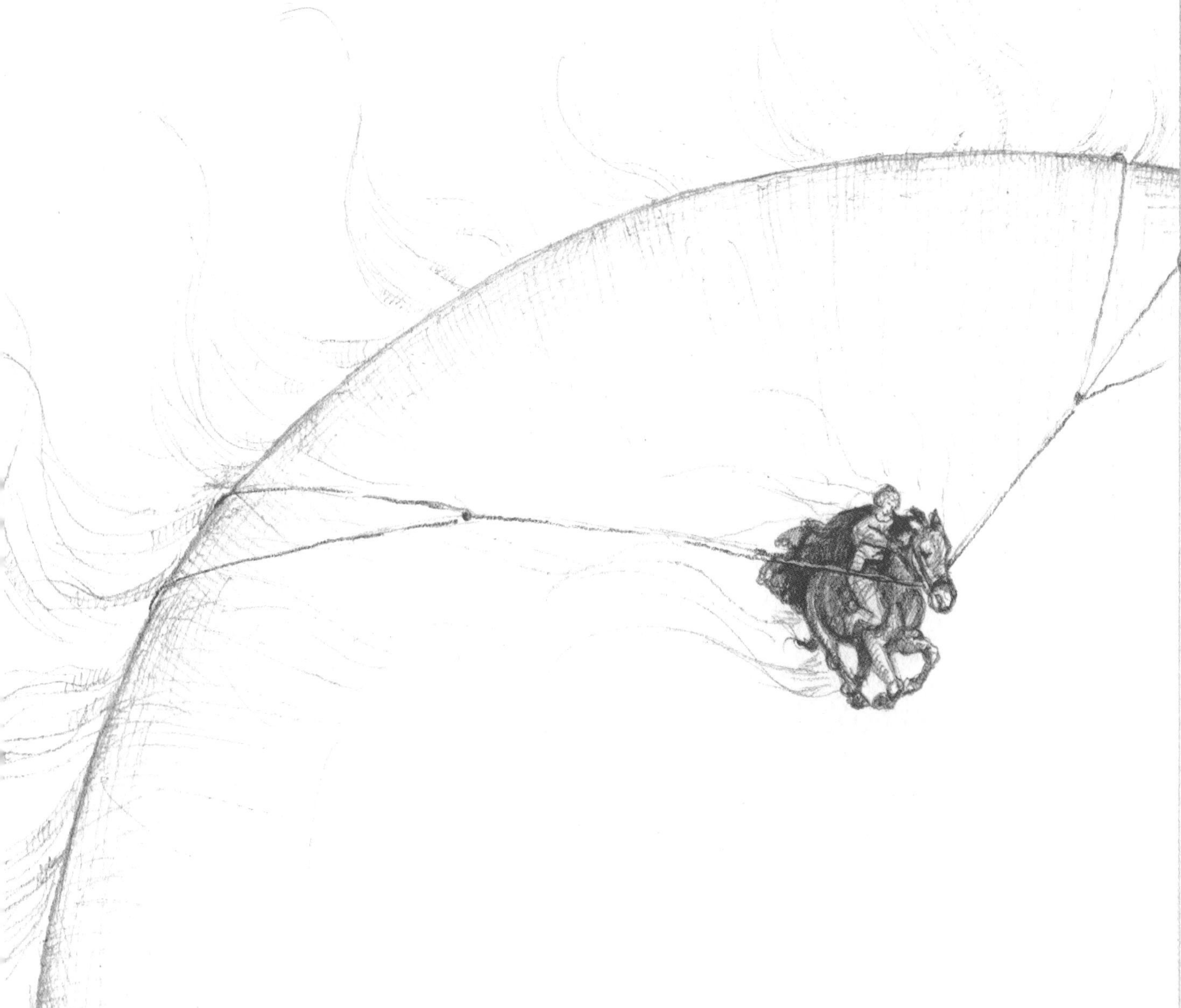

NYAI LORO KIDUL

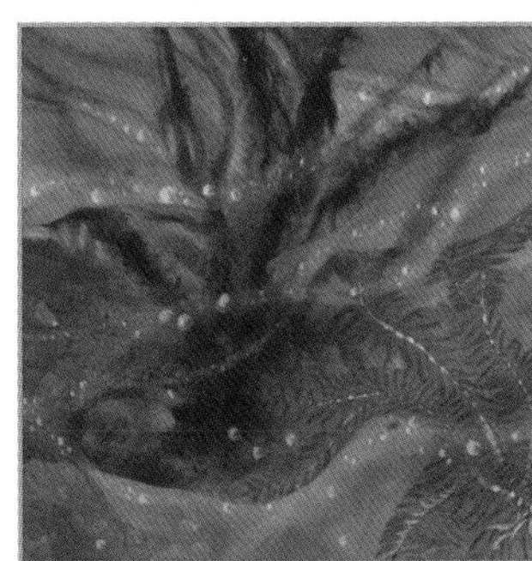

The royal family of the island of Java claims that their divine right to rule was bestowed on them by Nyai Loro Kidul, the mermaid goddess of the South Seas. One popular story says that this goddess married the king of Java in the sixteenth century. Before returning to the sea, she taught the king how to gain the power of the spirits, so that he could rule Java wisely. Since then, all rulers of Java have considered Nyai Loro Kidul their divine ancestress.

The story of Nyai Loro Kidul bears similarity to the well-known fairy tale of Cinderella. The goddess was once the mortal daughter of a king of Java in ancient times. Upon her mother's death, her father remarried unwisely. The princess's new stepmother was wildly jealous of her; with the aid of an evil wizard, she poisoned her stepdaughter's bathwater so that her skin erupted in permanent and painful sores. The poor disfigured princess was banished to the forests. She wandered there for a long time until she came to the south shore of the island.

While she rested on the ocean's edge, an ethereal voice called to her from beneath the moonlit waves. "Come and rest here," the voice said. "Here you shall be a mighty queen, regain your beauty, and rule the green ocean forever."

Immediately, the princess threw herself into the sea, where she was transformed into the radiant goddess Nyai Loro Kidul.

THE SEDUCTION OF THE SEA

The Javanese still honor Nyai Loro Kidul today. As a seductive mermaid queen, her powers reflect the mysterious, hidden forces of the ocean—forces that must be respected.

Local people know better than to swim in the waters on the south shore of Java, where the goddess is said to reside. It is believed that she looks out for mortals to serve her in her undersea realm and is especially enticed by young men wearing green bathing trunks. To appease the goddess, people leave offerings of coconuts, clothes, and fingernail clippings at the ocean's edge, all of which are eagerly accepted by the powerful sea.

Nyai Loro Kidul's story tells of passionate jealousies and miraculous transformations that heal the unhealable. Those who live to tell after encountering her speak of the mermaid goddess's undeniable power—a power as seductive as the fathomless sea.

GWENHYWFAR

In Wales, white-water waves are called "the sheep of the Mermaid." That mermaid is the goddess Gwenhywfar, who is honored as the first lady of the Welsh islands and sea. She is said to have existed for as long as there has been surf to pound against the rocky shore.

Some identify Gwenhywfar as the daughter of the first Welsh bard, the giant Ogyrvan. In Germany, she is called Cunneware, which means "female wisdom," and an early history mentions a Roman lady named Guanhumara. But today most people recognize Gwenhywfar as Queen Guinevere, the unhappy consort of King Arthur.

Guinevere was the daughter of King Leodegrance of the North. From the first moment King Arthur saw her willowy form, he knew he loved Guinevere and had to marry her. Arthur entrusted his most loyal knight, Lancelot du Lac, to present his suit to her. However, as soon as Lancelot's eyes met Guinevere's, they were possessed by a passion they could not control. Much as Guinevere respected her husband, it was Lancelot she desired; try as she might, she was torn between head and heart. The tragic triangle of Guinevere, Lancelot, and Arthur remained entrenched for the rest of their lives.

Queen Guinevere was responsible for the formation of the Knights of the Round Table. When she wed Arthur, Guinevere gave to her new husband a huge round oak table capable of seating one hundred and fifty knights. This round table was a wise gift, for while seated around it all knights were equal—none could sit higher or lower than any other.

The round table promoted peace among the warring knights, and became an emblem of the golden age of Camelot, the castle from which Arthur governed his realm. King Arthur and the Knights of the Round Table were famed for their brave and chivalrous deeds.

TO RULE OVER ALL

The story of Gwenhywfar reminds us of the strength necessary to make the right choices in our lives. If we are swayed by emotion, we run the risk of losing that which is closest to our hearts; if we are ruled by reason, we may find life without sweetness.

Since the goddess Gwenhywfar symbolized the throne of Wales, no king was able to rule without her by his side as his once and future queen. It is little wonder that many would-be kings attempted to abduct her. They foolishly thought that possessing the queen would make them king; they did not understand that it was Gwenhywfar's power that made them sovereign, not some romantic entanglement. Many of these myths worked their way into Arthurian legend, especially in the story of the struggle for the throne of Camelot. Mordred, the illegitimate son of Arthur, used the forbidden love of Lancelot for Guinevere to undermine the peaceful reign of his father.

In Welsh mythology, Arthur was born of Gwenhywfar when he was cast ashore by the ninth wave of the sea. When it was time for him to die, he was brought back into the sea by the goddess as she sang his death song. Welsh bards call such songs "giving back to the sea mother," or *marswygafen*. Other legends say that after Arthur's death, Gwenhywfar retreated to her castle, called Joyous Gard, where earthly paradise still exists. There she rules over her faithful subjects as Queen of the May each spring.

Artemis

RELATED GODDESSES

Cimidye

This Tucuna Indian goddess of the Amazon is associated with dragonflies and butterflies. Her myth of suffering and vengeance bears similarities to the story of Kuan Yin.

Cybele

In Phrygia, now part of modern Turkey, Cybele was honored as the Great Mother and as the Mistress of the Animals. She was traditionally represented with lions, who were often shown drawing her chariot. Each spring, this earth goddess was worshiped in wild, ecstatic rites that commemorated the death and rebirth of her consort, Attis.

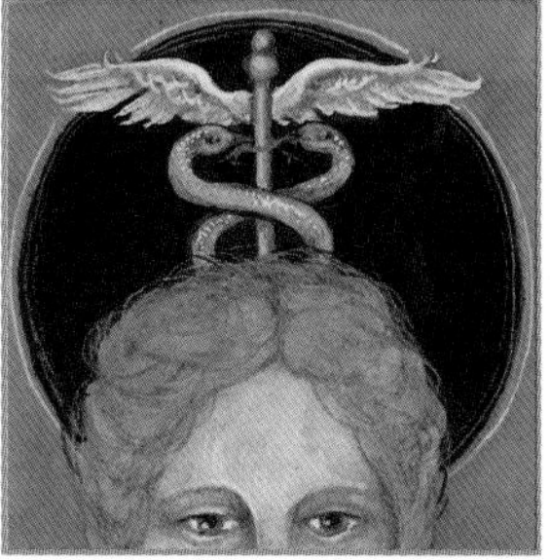

Hygeia

The goddess of health in ancient Crete, Hygeia was identified by a serpent. The serpent is a traditional symbol of renewal, suggesting the cycle of disease and healing.

Ogboinba

Daughter of the Nigerian mother goddess Woyengi, Ogboinba possessed magical abilities. While she was able to help the sick and foretell the future with these powers, they were not enough—Ogboinba yearned to become pregnant. Though she passed through seven kingdoms and risked death to gain this power, she was unsuccessful.

Saci

Also known as Indrani, Saci is the wife of Indra, the supreme ruling god during the Vedic period in early Hindu mythology. This goddess is renowned for her physical strength. Some accounts claim she bears one thousand eyes in her beautiful face.

Satyavati

In India, Satyavati was honored as a goddess of the truth. She was the daughter of Adrika, one of the Apsarases, or sacred water nymphs. However, the Sanskrit epic *Mahabharata* presents her as the mortal daughter of a ferryman. Later she becomes queen by marriage.

Sedna

Sedna was a mortal Inuit girl courted by many for her beauty. When she chose the supernatural Seabird as her husband, her father was infuriated. He sacrificed her to the sea, where she was transformed into a goddess who rules over all of the creatures who live within its depths. She is invoked by shamans and hunters to release the seals they yearn to hunt.

Sehkmet

This brave lion-headed Egyptian goddess was associated with the sun. Sehkmet is also a goddess of the underworld; as such, she is the goddess of strength, vengeance, and enchantments.

PART SIX

TRANSFORMATIONS

With beauty above me, I am traveling,
With my sacred power, I am traveling,
Now, with long life,
Now, with everlasting beauty, I live . . .

EXCERPT, BLESSINGWAY SONG

Inanna

AFTER THE TIME OF FERTILITY COMES THE TIME OF WISDOM. Hidden by the earth, the full moon has become dark. It is here that women are transformed into the all-powerful crone, a word thought to evolve from "crown." The crone is crowned with royalty, crowned with the divine knowledge of her age.

The crone has seen much and knows much. She knows how life begets death, and death begets life. The eternal cycle of the moon held magically within her body has ceased, having taught her all she needs to know. She knows she is courageous. She is wise. She is crone.

The goddesses described in this section encompass all types of transformations, from the darkness of the underworld to the light-giving circle of the sun. They reveal the magical powers that can lead us into the dark hollows of death and back again.

In a way, all goddesses are about transformations of one kind or another. For just as life is continually transforming, so are we, wise women all.

HEKATE

In ancient Greece, Hekate was honored as the Dark One, a mysterious goddess who brought visions and knowledge from the realm beyond life. As the wise crone aspect of the triple goddess, Hekate symbolizes the dark, or waning, moon—the time when the moon withholds its light before it illuminates the night sky once more. This phase of the moon is thought to symbolize the light held within all women—an inner light that can illuminate our own lives as well as others.

As goddess of the dark moon, Hekate was affiliated with storms, howling dogs, and willow trees, whose long, elegant branches often look like the arms of a supernatural being at night. The goddess is symbolized by a golden key, able to unlock untold riches from heaven and earth. In the famous story of Demeter and Persephone, it is Hekate who leads the bereft goddess to the sun god, Helios, thus reuniting mother and daughter.

Statues of Hekate were placed at crossroads, and depict her as a triple-headed elderly woman gazing out into the directions of past, present, and future. This image suggests the wisdom that later life can offer women. Having experienced so much, they can relax and share their lives' fruits with the world.

WELCOMING THE DARK MOON

For many women, menopause is a rebirth into a richly creative phase of life. No longer responsible for raising children, we are free to live for ourselves as we wish. But with rebirth comes death—the end of our ability to bear children, the finality of our youth. Both facets of this transformation must be acknowledged. The dark moon and Hekate, its goddess, are inspiring symbols for women undergoing this change of life.

In ancient times, women who had ceased their monthly flow were believed to hold their life-giving powers within themselves, like the dark moon. They were thought to be creating something powerful with their retained womb blood—pregnant with wisdom instead of new life. Valued and honored in their communities, these sage women had skills and powers no younger woman could possess. Like Hekate, they were crones, crowned with the intelligence of their years.

Hekate's festival was held on August thirteenth each year in Greece. Her worship was performed at the darkest hours of the night, often at places where three roads met. Divination was also performed in the goddess's name, no doubt because of her ability to discern the past, present, and future. Hekate's circle, a pendulum-like gold sphere containing a sapphire, was swung from a cord for answers to questions posed. Responses were deciphered from the direction and ferocity of movement.

Hekate was also invoked by offerings of food; these rituals were known as Hekate's suppers. Holly, a hardy evergreen, is also associated with Hekate. Its white flowers represent death; red berries, rebirth and life; and the bright green leaves, the hereafter. All three stages of life suggest the wide reach of Hekate's wisdom.

MAMAN BRIGITTE

The Voodoo faith is actively practiced in Haiti and other places throughout the Caribbean. Like Santeria, this religion was developed by African slaves forcibly brought to the new world to work upon plantations. The *loa*—spirits and divinities based on native Yoruba deities as well as forces of nature, who make up the Voodoo pantheon—are distinguished by characteristics inspired by their worshipers' experiences as enslaved people.

Among the *loa*, there are the Guédé, a supernatural family of approximately thirty death deities. The Guédé are thought to dress like undertakers, attired in dark formal clothing and glasses. To avoid inhaling the unsavory odors of rotting flesh, they plug their noses with cotton. One tale claims that these supernatural beings were raised from the dead by the powerful *loa*, Baron Samedi, and his wife, Maman Brigitte. It is because of this that Maman Brigitte is considered the mother of the Guédé.

An imposing, intense woman, the goddess often appears to her followers accompanied by a black rooster. She is thought to be fond of hot peppers and drum music. When Maman Brigitte honors the living with her presence, some claim she temporarily takes over their body to communicate with them—a phenomenon known as spirit possession. Those who are visited in this manner are considered to be blessed by her.

Besides being associated with death, Maman Brigitte is the goddess of cemeteries.

IN THE CITY OF DEATH

Ceremonies are potent reminders that life on earth is a transitory experience. Imbued with a mysterious, and sometimes frightening, atmosphere, these cities of the dead serve as homes to those

whose bodies have passed on. They are also the gateway to Guinee, the legendary Voodoo land where life begins and ends.

To gain entry to Guinee, the soul must pass the crossroad leading to it. Though the crossroad is patrolled by Baron Samedi, the cemetery is the realm of his wife, Maman Brigitte. Within it, the crossroad is symbolized by the numerous crosses dotting the somber landscape. These crosses are important, for it is believed that Maman Brigitte protects those whose graves have been memorialized by one; they enable the dead to enter the country of resurrection.

Other offerings are left alongside the crosses by the living: melted candles, ceremonial dolls, and food. All of these are designed to win the favor of Maman Brigitte, mother of the Guédé.

ARIANRHOD

Life and death are aspects of the same state. Neither can exist without the other, a duality hard to accept as long as we live and breathe. The shifting veil that separates these two states was envisioned by the Celts as an eternally turning silver wheel in the sky. The keeper of this wheel was Arianrhod, a mysterious death goddess who also ruled over the moon and fate. Some associate the silver wheel with the moon itself.

Mythology tells that Arianrhod was the most powerful daughter of Danu, the great Celtic mother goddess. She had two brothers, Gilfaethwy and Gwydion, who created trouble for Arianrhod when they started a war with Pryderi of Dyfed. Their exploits are retold in *The Mabinogion,* a collection of Welsh myths.

Arianrhod was pale of face, like the moon, and ethereal in appearance. She was responsible for bringing the souls of the dead to her castle, Caer Arianrhod, which was located in the *aurora borealis,* or northern lights. It was here that the dead waited for Arianrhod's eternal wheel to turn, bringing them the chance to be born to life again.

Others believe that the goddess's castle was located upon a long-forgotten island. Arianrhod and her ghostly handmaidens waited there to welcome the dead home from their lifelong journey. Some associate her mythical castle with a reef off the coast of England also called Caer Arianrhod.

THE SILVER WHEEL

Samhaim, the feast of Arianrhod, goddess of death, is celebrated every October thirty-first around the world. This holiday is also known as Hallowe'en, or All Hallows Eve, and exists in popular culture today as a children's holiday. It is on this evening that the veils separating life and death are thinnest—and the turning of Arianrhod's silver wheel can be sensed.

Many believe that on this evening the spirits of the dead roam the earth to bless or curse the living. To appease them, one ritual involved leaving offerings of food and wine. Some think it is from this that the present day tradition of trick-or-treating evolved. Samhaim is also the gateway to winter, the dark half of the year where night presides.

No matter how careful we may be in our relationships, when someone dies, we are often left with the burden of untied loose ends—words we wish we had said, sentiments unexpressed. Samhaim presents us with a wonderful opportunity for closure with those who have passed over to death, as well as those we may not be in contact with for whatever reason. It is a good time for the healing of wounds, for contemplating our own mortality.

The wisdom gained by this contemplation is the greatest gift Arianrhod can offer. It brings us the opportunity to appreciate all of life's precious sweetness before the goddess's silver wheel turns anew.

INANNA

Inanna, the great goddess of the Bronze Age, was honored with the title of Queen of Heaven. Some believed she was clothed with the stars, wearing the rainbow as a necklace, the zodiac as her belt, and the crescent moon as a crown upon her majestic head. As a sign of her divinity, Inanna is often depicted standing regally upon two winged lions. In Sumeria, where this goddess was worshiped five thousand years ago, her temple was called Eanna, which means "house of heaven."

Inanna had power over many aspects of Sumerian life. Besides ruling over the heavens, she was also goddess of the clouds which gave the rain necessary for grain to grow. Because the Sumerians believed that all moisture was caused by the moon, they considered the goddess responsible for the cool, lunar rays of light that carried precious dew to the earth during the night. Since Sumeria, known today as Iraq, is a land scorched by sun, it is understandable how valuable a goddess who created water would be.

Inanna's name translates as "Queen Moon." The story of her descent to the land of the dead explains her connection with that celestial body.

DESCENDING INTO THE DEPTHS

Inanna's older sister, Ereshkigal, was the goddess of death. She ruled over Kur-nu-gi-a, the land without return below the sweet waters of the earth. One day, Inanna descended to the land of the dead to visit her sister, who had lost her husband to that realm.

As the Queen of Heaven passed through each of the seven gates that led to the underworld, she was forced to give up a garment to gain passage. This unclothing of Inanna left the goddess defenseless

against attack—and with tragic results. Instead of showing her hospitality, Ereshkigal killed her sister and mercilessly hung her corpse upon a stake.

While Inanna was trapped within the land without return, the moon disappeared from the night sky; all things ceased to grow upon the earth. After three days, the water god obtained access to Inanna's corpse. He sprinkled it with the water of life, resurrecting Inanna, and she returned to the upper world, bringing the moon and all of life back with her. Another story claims that Inanna was freed when Dumuzi, her husband, offered to take her place in Kur-nu-gi-a.

One way to interpret this myth is that Inanna's trip to and from the land of the dead describes the waning and waxing of the moon. However, it also suggests the transformation all women face when they descend to the depths held within theirselves. As such, Ereshkigal symbolizes the darkest side of the psyche, what psychologist Carl Jung called "the shadow." However, Inanna's triumph over the forces of the underworld offers hope. If we face the darkness within, we will emerge reborn—just as the moon is born anew each cycle.

UKEMOCHI

The Japanese once believed that all the food of the earth was created by Ukemochi, a gentle and kind goddess. Because of Ukemochi's generosity, no one was ever short of food. The Japanese also thought that, instead of being separated by night and day, the sun and moon lived peacefully together in a palace in the heavens. This situation changed because of a task that was set to the moon god by the sun goddess Amaterasu.

One day Amaterasu commanded her brother, the moon god Tsuki-yomi, to go down to earth to visit Ukemochi and make certain that the food goddess was performing her duties correctly. Ukemochi was so excited and honored by Tsuki-yomi's rare visit that she prepared a grand feast for him. First, she turned her head to the land, and rice rushed forth from her mouth. Then she turned to the sea, and all kinds of fish spilled onto the banquet table, deliciously prepared for the moon god. Finally, Ukemochi turned toward the high mountains. Within moments, all sorts of meats emerged from her mouth and arranged themselves in as rich a feast as ever was, grander than anything the goddess had ever created for human or divinity.

But Tsuki-yomi was not impressed by Ukemochi's generous offering of food from her body—Tsuki-yomi was disgusted. He drew his sword and stabbed her. But even in death, Ukemochi was undeterred. She continued to create food. As she lay dying, her head turned into cows and horses, who ran off to populate the earth.

PROVIDING FOR OTHERS

From her sacrifice, Ukemochi's body lived on in many forms, providing nourishment for everyone. Grain sprouted from her forehead; its seed blew into the meadows and grew into vast fertile fields. Rice plants

sprouted from the goddess's belly, to bring plenty to all. Her inky eyebrows became silkworms, whose threads were woven into gloriously rainbow-colored silks to clothe the gods and goddesses.

When Amaterasu, the sun goddess, learned that her brother had killed Ukemochi, her fury was without limits at his violence. From that time on, the moon god has avoided being in the same place when Amaterasu is awake.

This Japanese story serves to explain why the sun is out during the day, and the moon only at night. It also suggests the traditional separation of women's work of providing for others from men's work outside the home.

Ukemochi's myth later became associated with the story of the Japanese rice deity, Inari. Associated with prosperity, Inari took on the form of a fox, and was considered both male and female. Other times the deity appeared as an older man with a long beard. Shrines to Inari can be found all over Japan, with the largest one located in Kyoto. Supplicants leave offerings of fried bean curd wrapped around rice to please the fox deity—just as Ukemochi left food to nurture the world, created from her divine body.

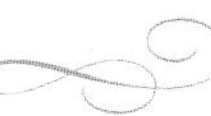

IDUNA

In ancient times, the Norse people considered apples essential for the continuation of life. Associated with the resurrection, containers of these sacred fruit were placed in graves, perhaps to nurture mortals as they journeyed from one life to the next. The Norse also believed that a soul could be passed from body to body, contained within the flesh of an apple. Many European folktales tell of infertile women who miraculously conceive a child after eating an apple.

Not surprisingly, the Norse credited the apple with granting eternal life to their deities. They honored Iduna as the goddess responsible for growing this fruit, which was eaten by the gods and goddesses to retain their youth and beauty. Iduna grew the golden apples of immortality in her enchanted western garden named Appleland; in the stories of King Arthur, Appleland was called Avalon—the idyllic country of immortal life.

Iduna was renowned for her youthful beauty, and was married to Bragi, the handsome god of poetry. As keeper of the golden apples, she was reponsible for the well-being of the Norse pantheon. Though she did her best to protect the gods and goddesses from harm, the mischievous fire god Loki nearly undermined their immortality.

STEALING YOUTH

Loki was always getting himself into trouble requiring the gods' intervention. One day, he was kidnapped by an eagle, who promised to free him if the god gave him Iduna in exchange. Since Loki lacked any scruples, he quickly agreed, and tricked Iduna. He told the goddess that he had found an orchard of golden apples, similar to the ones she grew. Naturally, Iduna was curious, so she followed Loki—

and was promptly snatched by the eagle, who took her far away from her beloved Appleland.

Without Iduna's apples, the gods' and goddesses' immortality was an illusion—they soon began to whither and age. Fortunately, they were able to convince Loki to rescue Iduna; the goddess Freya even volunteered her magical falcon skin, which enabled the wearer to fly through the sky. To escape the eagle, Loki turned Iduna into a walnut, which he successfully hid as they flew away. And so Iduna, goddess of youth, was restored to the gods and goddesses along with their youth.

HSI WANG MU

The people of China honor Hsi Wang Mu as the goddess of eternal life. Hsi Wang Mu lives in a golden palace on Jade Mountain, in a land called Kun-lun. Red phoenixes and white cranes, two birds that symbolize long life, are said to live there with her. Since Kun-lun is bordered on the west by a vast desert, only those who are invited may enter her domain.

But Hsi Wang Mu was not always the goddess of eternal life. Long ago, she was considered to be the bringer of plague and sickness. She was thought to have wild black hair, the savage teeth of a tiger, and the long tail of a leopard. Her only companions were three strange, green birds who flew across the world of humans to find food for her and bring it back to her dark and lonely cave.

It is uncertain how belief in Hsi Wang Mu transformed her from a goddess of death to a goddess of life. Today she is mainly remembered for her peaches—magical fruits that grant immortality to those who taste them.

THE FRUIT OF ETERNAL LIFE

The forbidden apple of wisdom that Eve tasted is the same fruit that has promised immortality around the world from time immemorial. Though in Scandinavia, divine Iduna offered apples to the gods and goddesses, in China peaches are given instead—delectable, magical peaches that create eternal life. These peaches, called *p'an t'ao* by the Chinese, were grown in Hsi Wang Mu's enchanted orchard, which was located in the lush gardens surrounding her heavenly realm in the Kun-lun Mountains.

It takes three thousand years for the peach trees in Hsi Wang Mu's enchanted orchard to come to fruit. During all this time, the goddess patiently tends them like a mother caring for her children; this

is why she is called the Royal Mother of the Western Paradise. The power of her peach trees is so remarkable that Chinese wizards used peach tree branches for magic wands.

When the peaches are finally ripe, Hsi Wang Mu invites all the Chinese gods and goddesses to a picnic to celebrate her birthday. Together they sit beside a magical fountain by a jewel-like lake and enjoy dish after dish of exotic foods such as bear paws, monkey lips, and dragon livers. After the last bite has been taken, Hsi Wang Mu serves the peaches to her guests. By eating the fruit, they can be sure that they will live for another three thousand years in good health and happiness.

Peaches are potent symbols of feminine power and sexuality. The sensual curves within their soft, dimpled flesh are evocative of a woman's form, and suggest the eternal fruitfulness of the universe. This unstoppable force of life was also celebrated during the Festival of the Moon, one of the three great annual Chinese holidays.

This festival, which also honors the moon goddess Chang O, takes place on the full moon of the autumnal equinox. It is a celebration of women and children. As people taste of the peaches, they are tasting life everlasting—the eternity offered by Hsi Wang Mu, Royal Mother of the Western Paradise.

CHANGING WOMAN

Changing Woman, also known as Estsanatlehi, is one of the most powerful deities of the Navajo Holy People. A benevolent fertility goddess, she is most often associated with corn, the grain that so many cultures rely upon for nourishment. Changing Woman symbolizes the ever-changing and ever-fertile earth. As suggested by her name, she appears as a young maiden for the spring and summer, and transforms into an old woman for the fall and winter.

According to Navajo myth, Changing Woman was first discovered by human beings. A gray rain cloud led the first man and woman to the summit of a mountain, where they found the goddess. She was fed pollen by the sun and grew to be a woman in only eighteen days. Later, she became the wife of the sun. The Navajo believe that the sun visits her every evening at her sacred home, set in the west upon the great water.

Changing Woman's home is surrounded by four mountains, replicas of the north, south, east, and west boundaries of the Navajo nation. By dancing on each one in turn, she creates rain clouds from the eastern mountain, and beautiful fabrics and jewels from the southern. Her dance upon the western mountain provides plants of all kinds, while her northern dance creates corn and animals.

THE CIRCLE OF LIFE

Changing Woman generously taught humans how to control the elements of nature. Her teachings are presented within the Blessingway, a group of essential rituals and chants she is believed to have authored. The songs and ceremonies that make up the Blessingway are used for weddings, childbirth rites, and other happy occasions in the life of the Navajo. Each Blessingway takes place over several days

and includes many songs, prayers, and ceremonial baths in yucca, or cactus, suds. Pulverized flower blossoms, cornmeal, and pollen are spread upon the earth to bless it and to bring good fortune.

The Kinaalda is a major part of the Blessingway rituals. Like the cycle of life that Changing Woman represents, the Kinaalda honors one of the most important points of a woman's life—her transformation from girl to woman. For young women who have just experienced their first menstruation, it is a way for the Navajo to celebrate their maturity. By participating in the Kinaalda, young women are blessed with the generous, life-affirming wisdom of Changing Woman, and readied for their new roles as women in their community.

The Kinaalda is held over a four-day period. The young girl honored is dressed in a special costume and her hair is pulled back to evoke the sand painting depictions of Changing Woman. As if they are molding her character as well as her body, elder women of the tribe massage the girl's body; it is believed that at this time the girl's body is as soft as a newborn's.

Perhaps the most important part of the Kinaalda takes place on the final day. This is when the Alkaan, an immense ceremonial cake, is finally eaten. During the earlier part of the Kinaalda, the corn for this cake has been ground by the young girl. As the Alkaan is baked in a pit, it is sprinkled with ceremonial cornmeal and covered with husks. Singing is heard as it cooks overnight:

With beauty before me, I am traveling,
With my sacred power, I am traveling,
With beauty behind me, I am traveling,
With my sacred power, I am traveling.

Traditionally, the Alkaan cake baked during the Kinaalda represents Mother Earth. It is offered to the sun as thanks for its help in growing the corn sacred to Changing Woman, goddess of the fertile earth.

Maman Brigitte

RELATED GODDESSES

Baba Yaga

Many of us think of Baba Yaga as an evil, child-eating witch with a home set upon chicken claws, which is how she is traditionally presented in Russian fairy tales. Originally this goddess represented the life cycle, from birth to death. In Hungarian folklore, she was initially acknowledged as a good fairy.

Coatlicue

Sovereign over the primal states of life and death, Coatlicue was mother to all the Aztec gods and goddesses. She wore a skirt made of living serpents, as terrifying as her dark, wrinkled face. One story tells that she became pregnant with the war god, Huitzilopochtli, after tucking a ball of feathers against her breast. Coatlicue also ruled over the stars.

Isamba

This goddess of Tanzania was originally associated with the moon. One folktale relates how she became the creator of death.

Kali Ma

This Hindu triple goddess is widely worshiped in India. Acceptance of Kali Ma the Destroyer recognizes that life cannot exist without death; death allows an opportunity for new growth to rise from the old.

Mebuyan

In Burma, Mebuyan is the goddess of death and the underworld. It is thought that she creates life and death by shaking the tree of life, as if harvesting fruit from a tree.

The Moirae

In ancient Greece, the Moirae were the three Fates, spinners of destiny. As such, they were responsible for the creation, preservation, and destruction of life, much like other triple goddesses honored around the world.

Myesyats

Similar to the Navajo deity Changing Woman, this Slavic goddess ages during the year to reflect the different ages of women. Myesyats is associated with the moon and time.

Pajau Yan

This Vietnamese goddess of healing is associated with lunar eclipses and is often worshiped on the first day of the waning moon. Pajau Yan is often invoked for good fortune and health.

SOURCE NOTES AND BIBLIOGRAPHY

The art and words offered in *The Book of Goddesses* are the product of many hours of work and research. I wove the goddesses' stories from various sources, and in doing so searched for an illustrative approach that would honor each tradition. I decided that the best way to do this would be to depict the goddesses as women, with the clothing, jewelry, and demeanor appropriate to the culture that honored them.

Books by their nature are collaborative ventures: I cannot imagine how I could have written this one without the help of the following. Indispensible and comprehensive, Barbara Walker's *The Women's Encyclopedia of Myths and Secrets,* Martha Ann and Dorothy Myers Imel's *Goddesses in World Mythology,* and Patricia Monaghan's *The Book of Goddesses and Heroines* were supremely helpful to me, especially with the shorter descriptions of the lesser known goddesses; these books deserve a place in the library of any goddess or mythology enthusiast. I must also mention Carolyne Larrington's *The Feminist Companion to Mythology* and Merlin Stone's *When God Was a Woman*—their books are treasures for women everywhere. On the web, the comprehensive Encyclopedia Mythica (www.pantheon.org) was of immense aid.

Several of the quotes beginning each section of this book were taken from Elaine Partnow's *The New Quotable Woman: The Definitive Treasury of Notable Words by Women from Eve to the Present,* an astonishing collection of women's wit and wisdom. They include the fragment of poetry by Sappho (page 26), the poem from *The Confessions of Lady Nijo,* which was translated by Karen Brazell (page 104), and the quote from Anaïs Nin's *Diaries* (page 52). The excerpts from the Blessingway ritual song (page 134 and 155) were found in Karen Liptak's *Coming-of-Age: Traditions and Rituals from Around the World.* The excerpt from the *Mahalakshmi Stotram* ("Hymn to Lakshmi," page 76) is, as far as I could ascertain, a traditional Hindu prayer, as is the prayer to Sarasvati (page 97). The Orphic hymn to Gaia (page 7) was translated by Virginia Stewart, M. Ed. Every effort has been made to acknowledge the copyright holders of previously published materials.

A selected bibliography follows. I hope that these books will inspire you to learn more about the Divine Feminine and her nurturing, healing influence.

Ann, Martha, and Dorothy Myers Imel. *Goddesses in World Mythology.* Oxford University Press, 1993.

Baring, Anne, and Jules Cashford. *The Myth of the Goddess.* Viking Books, 1992.

Bascom, William. *The Yoruba of Southwestern Nigeria.* Holt, Rinehart, and Winston, 1969.

Beier, Ulli. *Yoruba Myths.* Cambridge University Press, 1980.

Bell, Robert E. *Women of Classical Mythology: A Biographical Dictionary.* Oxford University Press, 1993.

Bierhorst, John. *The Mythology of North America.* Quill/William Morrow, 1985.

Bolen, Jean Shinoda. *Goddesses in Everywoman: A New Psychology of Women.* HarperCollins, 1985.

—. *Goddesses in Older Women: Archetypes in Women over Fifty.* HarperCollins, 2001.

Brown, Karen McCarthy. *Mama Lola: A Vodou Priestess in Brooklyn.* University of California Press, 1991.

Bulfinch, Thoms. *Bulfinch's Mythology.* Signet/New American Library, 1962.

Burland, Cottie. *North American Indian Mythology.* Peter Bedrick Books, 1985.

Campbell, Joseph. *The Masks of God: Primitive Mythology.* Arkana/Penguin USA, 1987.

Carlyon, Richard. *A Guide to the Gods.* Quill/William Morrow, 1981.

Carmody, Denise Lardner. *Mythological Woman: Contemporary Reflections on Ancient Religious Stories.* Crossroad Publishing Company, 1992.

Christie, Anthony. *Chinese Mythology.* Hamlyn Publishing Group, 1968.

Crossley-Holland, Kevin. *The Norse Myths.* Pantheon Fairy Tale and Folklore Library, 1980.

D'Aulaire, Ingri, and Edgar Parin. *D'Aulaire's Norse Gods and Giants.* Doubleday, 1967.

Davidson, H. R. Ellis. *Myths and Symbols in Pagan Europe: Early Scandinavian and Celtic Religions.* Syracuse University Press, 1988.

Downing, Christine, editor. *The Long Journey Home: Re-visioning the Myth of Demeter and Persephone for Our Time.* Shambhala, 1994.

Eliade, Mircea. *Birth and Rebirth: The Religious Meanings of Initiation in Human Culture.* Harper and Brothers, 1958.

—. *Images and Symbols: Studies in Religious Symbolism.* Princeton University Press, 1991.

Erdoes, Richard, and Alfonso Ortiz, editors. *American Indian Myths and Legends.* Pantheon Books, 1984.

Frazer, Sir James G. *The Golden Bough: A Study in Magic and Religion.* The MacMillion Company, 1958.

Gadon, Elinor W. *The Once and Future Goddess.* Harper and Row, 1989.

Gimbutas, Marija. *The Goddesses and Gods of Old Europe, 6500-3500 B.C. Myths and Cult Images.* University of California Press, 1982.

Gonzalez-Wippler, Migene. *The Santeria Experience.* Original Publications, 1982.

Grahn, Judy. *Blood, Bread, and Roses: How Menstruation Created the World.* Beacon Press, 1993.

Grant, Michael. *Myths of the Greeks and Romans.* Harry N. Abrams, 1962.

Grimal, Pierre, editor. *Larousse World Mythology.* Hamlyn Publishing Group, 1968.

Harding, M. Esther. *Woman's Mysteries: Ancient and Modern.* Harper Perennial Library, 1976.

Hooke, S. H. *Middle Eastern Mythology: From the Assyrians to the Hebrews.* Penguin Books, 1963.

Hubbs, Joanna. *Mother Russia: The Feminine Myth in Russian Culture.* Indiana Univesity Press, 1988.

Issacs, Jennifer. *Arts of the Dreaming: Australia's Living Heritage.* Weldon Publishing, 1990.

Jaffrey, Madhur. *Seasons of Splendor: Tales, Myths, and Legends of India.* Puffin Books, 1987.

Ke, Yuan. *Dragons and Dynasties: An Introduction to Chinese Mythology.* Penguin Books, 1993.

Kluckhorn, Clyde, and Dorothea Leighton. *The Navaho.* Doubleday Anchor, 1962.

Kraemer, Ross Shepard. *Her Share of the Blessings: Woman's Religions Among Pagans, Jews, and Christians in the Greco-Roman World.* Oxford University Press, 1992.

Kramer, Samuel Noah. *Mythologies of the Ancient World.* Anchor Books, 1961.

Larrington, Carolyne, editor. *The Feminist Companion to Mythology.* Pandora/HarperCollins, 1992.

Lehmann, Arthur C., and James E. Myers. *Magic, Witchcraft, and Religion: An Anthropological Study of the Supernatural.* Mayfield Publishing Company, 1985.

Leonard, Linda Scierse. *On the Way to the Wedding: Transforming the Love Relationship.* Shambhala, 1986.

Liptak, Karen. *Coming-of-Age: Traditions and Rituals from Around the World.* The Millbrook Press, 1994.

Locke, Raymond Friday. *The Book of the Navajo.* Mankind Publishing Company, 1992.

MacCana Proinsias. *Celtic Mythology.* Peter Bedrick Books, 1983.

McNeely, Jeffrey A., and Paul Spencer Wachtel. *Soul of the Tiger.* Doubleday, 1988.

Monaghan, Patricia. *The Book of Goddesses and Heroines.* Llewellyn Publications, 1993.

Nicholson, Irene. *Mexican and Central American Mythology.* Hamlyn Publishing Group, 1969.

Nicholson, Shirley. *The Goddess Re-awakening.* Quest Books, 1989.

Osborne, Harold. *South American Mythology.* Hamlyn Publishing Group, 1969.

Parrinder, Geoffrey. *African Mythology.* Hamlyn Publishing Group, 1969.

Partnow, Elaine, editor. *The New Quotable Woman: The Definitive Treasury of Notable Words by Women from Eve to the Present.* Meridien Books/Penguin USA, 1993.

Perowne, Stewart. *Roman Mythology.* Peter Bedrick Books, 1988.

Piggot, Juliet. *Japanese Mythology.* Peter Bedrick Books, 1991.

Pomeroy, Sarah B. *Goddesses, Whores, Wives, and Slaves: Women in Classical Antiquity.* Shocken Books, 1975.

Rush, Anne Kent. *Moon, Moon.* Random House/Moon Books, 1976.

Rutherford, Ward. *Celtic Lore: The History of the Druids and Their Timeless Traditions.* HarperCollins, 1993.

Sander, Tao Tao Lui. *Dragons, Gods and Spirits from Chinese Mythology.* Peter Bedrick Books, 1980.

Sered, Susan Starr. *Priestess, Mother, Sacred Sister: Religions Dominated by Women.* Oxford University Press, 1994.

Shearer, Alistair. *Forms of the Formless: The Hindu Vision.* Thames and Hudson, 1993.

Spence, Lewis. *The Illustrated Guide to Native American Myths and Legends.* Longmeadow Press, 1993.

Spretnak, Charlene. *Lost Goddesses of Early Greece.* Beacon Press, 1992.

Starck, Marcia, and Gynne Stein. *The Dark Goddess: Dancing With the Shadow.* The Crossing Press, 1993.

Starhawk. *The Spiral Dance.* HarperCollins, 1979.

Stone, Merlin. *Ancient Mirrors of Womanhood.* Beacon Press, 1991.

—. *When God Was a Woman.* Harvest/Harcourt Brace Jovanovich Books, 1976.

Sykes, Egerton. *Who's Who in Non-Classical Mythology.* Oxford University Press, 1993.

Walker, Barbara G. *The Crone: Woman of Age, Wisdom, and Power.* HarperSanFrancisco, 1985.

—. *The Women's Encyclopedia of Myths and Secrets.* HarperSanFrancisco, 1983.

—. *Women's Rituals: A Sourcebook.* HarperCollins, 1990.

Wolkstein, Diane. *The First Love Stories.* HarperCollins, 1991.

Young, Serinity, editor. *An Anthology of Sacred Texts by and about Women.* Crossroad Publishing Company, 1993.

INDEX

GODDESSES